Stamping**Tricks**
for Scrapbooks

ROCKPORT

First published in the
United States of America by
Rockport Publishers, Inc.
33 Commercial Street
Gloucester, Massachusetts 01930-5089
Telephone: 978-282-9590
Fax: 978-283-2742
www.rockpub.com

ISBN 1-56496-847-2
10 9 8 7 6 5 4 3 2 1
Design: Leeann Leftwich Zajas
Photography: Brian Piper Photography

Printed in China

GLOUCESTER MASSACHUSETTS

Stamping **Tricks** *for* Scrapbooks

ROCKPORT PUBLISHERS

A Guide for Enhancing
Your Pages with Stamps

Betty Auth

Contents

Introduction

As an art form develops over time, it seems to become more and more sophisticated and refined. The artists who work within a particular medium become more adept at designing and at using their tools. Choices become more numerous as the availability of materials begins to grow. More artists are attracted to the medium, and they bring other skills and methods with them, so the range of supplies and techniques increases even more.

This has happened with rubber stamping. More people are creating within this discipline, and more companies are producing better and better designs and products for us to use. This has also happened with scrapbooks and memory products. As more people are attracted to preserving and beautifully presenting their family photographs, more companies are making more diverse and refined scrapbooking products.

These two areas are now on the verge of a merge. Stampers want new ways to use their stock of stamps and accessories, and scrapbook enthusiasts want new ideas for building their libraries of memory pages.

This book meets the needs of both groups by concentrating on artful scrapbooks made with stamps. If you're a stamper who has yet to try scrapbooking, you will find lots of help and inspiration to get started. If, on the other hand, you're a scrapbooker who is searching for new ideas for artistic albums, you'll see how stamps can be used to meet that need.

If you are neither a stamper nor a scrapbooker, but want to try these art forms, this book will start you in the right direction by showing you some of the most beautiful uses of both mediums.

The key to creativity is experimentation. I believe that each of us is creative, that it is built into our systems to be so. We have a need to create in order to fulfill the purpose that each of us carries throughout life. To go along with that belief, I think the most joy and happiness comes with the surprises that occur when we try something new.

So leaf through, start anywhere, and try the techniques. We tell you what we did to create the pages within the chapters, knowing that you will add your own personal flair through your selection of photos and techniques. Mix and match, or make your pages as close to the artists' methods as possible – it really doesn't matter. Just start and, most of all, enjoy the creative process.

Each chapter begins with the easiest or simplest pages, then we add a little to each successive page. The first few chapters are also the simplest and most basic, and they progress to the more complex as you work through the book. However, it all depends upon your level of expertise in any given technique, so the later chapters may be the ones you find the easiest. Again, it doesn't matter where you start, so choose something that appeals to you and try it. Enjoy the act of making art.

Betty Auth

the basics

Basics

Most of the tools and techniques in this book are very simple, but a few of the pages will take a little practice. The key to success is experimentation, and there are many techniques for you to try. Each chapter begins with the easiest projects and progresses to more complex pages. All the pages are within reach of the average stamping enthusiast or scrapbooking beginner.

To Make the Page at Left

Use paper edgers to trim a 2" – 3" (5 cm – 8 cm) strip from the end of a sheet of lime green cardstock, and apply it over the top edge of a darker green sheet. Use an allover flower-patterned block stamp to emboss the whole page in bronze. Stamp and emboss the letters on lime green cardstock, then cut them out with the paper edgers. Tear a rectangle of handmade blue and green paper and glue it a little above the center of the green cardstock. Glue the letters to the handmade paper. A pair of long-handled tweezers is handy for precisely placing the letters.

BASIC STAMPING TOOL KIT

- ## Stamps
  Variety of images and sizes
  Alphabets

- ## Inks and Inkpads
  Dye-and pigment-based inkpads and reinkers
  Clear and tinted embossing inks and powders

- ## Adhesives
  Two-way glue pen
  Photo squares
  Paper adhesive
  Glue stick
  Removable tape

- ## Cutting tools
  Paper trimmer
  Paper edgers
  Straight blade 5" (13 cm) precision scissors
  Craft knife with extra blades
  Paper punches

- ## Measuring and aligning tools
  Transparent ruler marked in squares
  Cork-backed metal ruler
  Stamp positioner (optional)

- ## Papers
  Assorted cardstock in your favorite colors
  Handmade papers in a variety of textures
  Metallic and holographic sheets
  Inexpensive copy paper (the least expensive is
  usually the most absorbent)

- ## Drawing and planning tools
  No. 2 pencils, very sharp
  Art gum and white erasers
  Soft brush for eliminating eraser dust
  Fine-point black permanent marker

- ## Miscellaneous tools
  Stamp cleaner (spray or scrubber bottle)
  Long-handled tweezers
  Wooden skewers
  Heat tool for embossing
  Protective cutting mat
  Ink brayer or roller

photographs

The projects in this book might be considered art scrapbooks, and as such they utilize techniques and materials that are not always of archival quality. For that reason, you should not use your only copy of a photograph on the pages—save your priceless photographs in archival-safe storage boxes. If you have access to a home computer with a good photo program and printer, use it with photographic paper or good copy paper to copy the photos. Today's copy centers and photo centers can be a great source of help with copying photographs in a variety of ways, and the personnel at these centers can often advise you on the best methods for obtaining great copies.

materials

The artists whose pages are presented here have used a wide range of stamping and scrapbooking materials for each project. Check the Resources section on page 104 for contact information about these products. In addition, you will need a basic kit of materials for constructing the pages. You may have most of these materials already, and others that work for you. The list at left is merely a suggested list of items that are handy to have on hand. By all means, substitute your own if you like.

stamping

Most of the stamping in this book is done with commercially purchased rubber stamps. They are readily available in stamp and craft stores, and through mail order and on-line merchants. You will find contact information for these companies in the Resources section on page 104.

   Commercially manufactured rubber stamps come in an unlimited variety of styles, sizes, themes, and forms. The most common type is red rubber that has been mounted on a wooden block with the image illustrated on the opposite side (top) of the block. Some stamps are made of clear vinyl and mounted on Lucite blocks so you can see where you are stamping the image. Some stamps are sold unmounted, by the page; you can cut them apart and mount them yourself. You can also make your own stamps by carving into white erasers, foam blocks, potatoes, cork, and specially formulated stamp-carving blocks of linoleum or soft rubber.

   To stamp an image, first pat the rubber side of the stamp on an inkpad or turn it rubber-side up and pat the stamp with the pad. Use an art pad, not an office inkpad. Pat until all the ridges are covered with ink. Turn it over and stamp gently on a sheet of non-glossy paper without moving the stamp once it has touched the surface. Let the stamp rest for a couple of seconds, then press over the entire wooden block with your fingertips to transfer the image. Lift the stamp directly up to avoid smears.

   When finished stamping, or when changing colors, use a stamp cleaner to remove the ink and wipe with a paper towel. Baby wipes can be used as well, and glass cleaner in a spray bottle will work in a pinch. Don't immerse the stamps in water, or the adhesive may loosen and the stamp will come off the block. Always dry your stamps after cleaning and store them out of direct sunlight.

Keep your clean and dry stamps rubber-side down in a shallow container for easy access and prolonged life. Map chests with many shallow drawers are an excellent storage place for stamps. With care, your stamps will last for many years.

embossing

Embossed stamps are created with embossing ink, embossing powder, and heat with an embossing tool. Embossing inks are available clear, or with a tint so you can see where they have been stamped on the page. The tint will be covered completely, so its color will not show after embossing. The ink is sticky and stays moist longer than most other inks, but you need to work quickly for the best results. You may use pigment inks for embossing, although they don't stay moist quite as long as embossing inks and the result may not be as satisfactory.

To emboss an image, place your art paper on a large protective sheet of newsprint, cardboard, or other protective paper, then stamp with embossing ink. While the ink is wet, sprinkle liberally with embossing powder, covering all the ink. Check the labels for any special precautions or directions such as those found on extra-thick powders that are not recommended for detailed stampings. Pick up the sprinkled art paper and pour the extra powder back into the original container, tapping the paper to loosen the excess powder. This may be a lot easier with the help of a Tidy Tray (see Resources, page 104), which has a funnel built into one end just for this purpose. Turn on the heat tool and move it slowly across the embossing powder, holding the tool a few inches above the surface. The stamping will change before your eyes, and you can see when it's "done" because the powder will melt as you heat it.

There are many advanced techniques for embossing, and again the key is experimentation. Try new methods on scrap papers or cards before using them on your scrapbook pages.

tearing paper

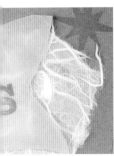

To create a ragged edge, use deckle paper edgers, or try tearing the paper. To tear, place a ruler on top of the paper where you want it torn and pull the excess paper up toward you while holding the ruler firmly in place. Different papers tear differently, and there are many metal and plastic rulers with deckle and other shapes made specifically for this edge treatment. Experiment on some blank papers, and try different tearing angles. To

simulate an aged look, sponge or lightly brush brown ink along the edges after tearing. Further age the appearance by wadding the paper then flattening it out to cause creasing.

shadow stamping

Although some artists define "shadow stamping" as the application of pale squares of color to a background, the term has evolved to include many other techniques. Before stamping an image, use the same stamp and very pale dye ink to create a shadow slightly to the right and below the position where the main image will go. Reink the stamp with pigment ink and stamp it over the shadow, allowing the shadow to show. For another method of shadow stamping, use pale inks on a background sheet to randomly stamp an image, then use a slightly darker color to stamp over the first impressions. Continue darkening or brightening the color as you stamp consecutive layers of the image, always allowing the palest images to show. This will create depth and interest.

faux batik

Batik is a decorative method traditionally used on fabric, but it can also be used on paper with a few simple modifications. Here is one method to try. On glossy cardstock, draw some linear designs with an Easter egg decorating crayon. (These are made with a much harder wax than the usual art crayons, and will form a better resist on paper.) After drawing the designs, paint or stamp some pigment inks over them. Place the paper on newsprint or several layers of paper towel, cover it with a sheet of typing paper to protect the surface of the iron, then iron the surface of the paper to melt the crayon. The paper will remain blank wherever the wax was applied.

monoprinting

Monoprints make beautiful and interesting backgrounds and middle grounds, as well as embellishments for scrapbook pages. They are one-of-a-kind artist prints that are much easier to create than their lofty name implies. The name "monoprint" is appropriate because each print is a single impression printed from paint or ink applied to a printing plate. For the pages in this book, the printing plate is a sheet of flexible vinyl and the color is often obtained from an inkpad or reinker. See page 21 for methods and illustration of the technique.

GLUES AND ADHESIVES

Adhesives and glues that clean up with water are the best for paper because they are safe, convenient, and require no solvents. There are four basic types of adhesives for scrapbooks, and they come in several forms. The main types are dry, wet, heated, and sprays.

Dry adhesives include glue sticks, photo stickers and corners, and mounting tapes and sheets.

Wet adhesives may be applied with a brush or a toothpick, and some brands have fine-pointed applicators in their lids. Wet adhesives that are in liquid form may be thinned with water, or you can let them sit in an open container or saucer to thicken them. Easy-to-use glue pens resemble chisel point markers filled with glue instead of ink.

Heated glue is available in sticks that fit into glue guns. Sticks and chips can also be heated in electric dipping pots for large items. These pots were developed for the floral industry and are not generally recommended for paper projects because they are messy and the glue can leave a bumpy surface when cool.

Spray adhesives can be a good choice for mounting photos and other papers. Read the instructions to see if the glue sets immediately or if it needs to dry first. If possible, spray outdoors, using long-handled tweezers to hold and manipulate the item. Spray lightly on the back of a photo or paper shape. (Excess spraying is messy.)

stamp carving

There are many new products made specifically for carving stamps, including carving tools with comfortable wooden handles and interchangeable points. Some stamp carving materials are shown in the photograph on page 49. There are several sizes and types of carving blocks in craft and stamp stores, and these blocks are as easy as butter to cut. You can cut a stamp-carving block with a craft knife to make it a manageable size, and you can carve images on the front, the back, and even the edges. Start by lightly penciling a design onto the block—remember that it will be a mirror image of the impression—and then carve away the background. Use knitting needles, kitchen tools, awls, and other implements to make your carvings unique. Start with a simple design. You can draw it first on plain paper then use graphite paper to transfer the image to the block. You can also draw a design on paper, cut it out, and trace around it onto the block. Always try your hand-carved stamps on scrap paper first, to be sure the lines are clear and the background has been deeply carved.

craft knife cutting

It's always best to use a self-healing cutting mat with your craft knife. It will protect the work surface and make it easier to cut all the way through paper or matte board. If possible, stand up while cutting with a craft knife, and always use a sharp blade. To cut a straight line, use a cork-lined metal ruler and pull the knife toward you along its edge. For foam core or thick matte board, score the surface first, then go over the score lines with hard pressure.

paper edgers

There are dozens of decorative edges available in scissors-like paper edgers. Try a few in a variety of designs to get started, then add to your collection as you go. For the best results with these edgers, begin by cutting out a photograph or a shape with straight scissors or a craft knife just a little larger than you wish the finished piece to be, then trim the straight edge with the decorative blades. Cut almost to the end of the blade, then reset your edgers, matching up the curves in the blades with the part you've already cut, and finish the edge a little at a time.

air-dry modeling clay

When you need a special stamp shape, make your own from clay. A modeling compound made for kids will air-dry overnight with very little shrinkage, and it remains flexible (see Resources, page 104). Knead this moist, white clay and roll it out between sheets of waxed paper to about ⅛" to ¼" (3 mm to 5 mm) thick. Use cookie cutters or a craft knife to form the shapes you want, then score them and add texture with a stylus. You can also impress the clay surface with things found around the house such as a tea strainer, a cheese grater, carved jewelry, pressed glass, or other object. Let the clay shapes dry overnight, then ink them and use as stamps. This technique is shown in the journal on page 78.

sponges

Natural kitchen and cosmetic sponges make interesting impressions, particularly for backgrounds. Dip them into paint or tap on an inkpad and apply to paper or cardstock. Use them as they come, or pinch off bits to create the shape needed or to disguise the straight edges of the sponges. Keep the sponge shapes simple and always try them out on scrap paper first.

mica chips

Mica chips, or embossing tiles, are available in large, intermediate, and small sizes. You can cut them, stamp on them, foil or paint them, or just enjoy them without altering their surface. Glue them on or drill holes and attach with screws or fine coiled wire. Transparent pieces of mica were used on the travel journal on page 90.

coloring techniques and tools

Colored pencils come in many forms, including oil, chalk, watercolor, and more. All are valuable tools for adding color to your pages, and most are sold with some instruction. Try them all and find the ones that you like best. Great backgrounds can also be created with direct stamping methods by lightly applying small cube or other inkpads directly to the cardstock or paper, using a slight twisting motion. This technique can be combined with brushing or sponging more ink over the top, or using daubers to refine the color on the page.

mesh

You can use metal screen from the hardware store, plastic canvas mesh, and various mesh materials from your kitchen or garage to create interesting patterns by spraying or daubing ink through the holes. The project on pages 70 and 71 is a beautiful example of this method. Meshes in a variety of patterns are available in stamp specialty stores and through on-line merchants.

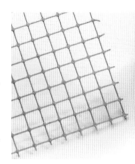

lettering methods

A variety of alphabet stamps are available, and their number is growing every day. Some are good for creating words and phrases because of their size and simplicity, and others are highly decorative, reminiscent of ancient illuminated manuscripts. You will find examples of both in the lettering chapter. Some of the most charming pages are those that include hand lettering. Your family and friends will treasure those pages the most because they impart a bit of yourself and they show that you care enough to take extra time. The quickest and easiest lettering method may be letter stickers or rub-ons, and with a little extra attention they can be very effective. Try embellishing them with stamps and dyes, and place shadow backgrounds around them with chalk or sponged ink.

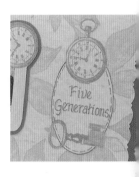

Creating Layouts

There are thousands of possibilities for layouts on scrapbook pages, and a great number of ideas are presented in this book. The main element of a good scrapbook layout is simplicity. Even though the techniques may be complicated and embellishments applied layer after layer, the basic framework should remain simple.

Study the examples in the various chapters and notice how the page elements relate to one another, then adapt them to your own pages even if the themes are entirely different.

If you are designing a double-page spread where both pages are visible at once, plan the layout so some of the elements cross over from the left page to the right. This will help tie the two pages together and make them more cohesive.

To Make the Page at Left

Use a gold cat's-eye inkpad to stamp directly on a sheet of deep lavender cardstock, swirling the pad as you go over the page. Sponge on some burgundy pigment ink in the same way, folding the sponge to eliminate straight edges. Stamp the large, lacy leaves with purple pigment ink. Stamp the letters with purple ink on red cardstock and cut them out with paper edgers. Glue the letters onto a piece of gold cardstock and cut it into the shape of a banner. With a paintbrush and a dark neutral chalk or ink, stipple some shadows under the letters. Glue the banner onto the background.

QUICK TRICK

Make some inexpensive black and white copies of your photographs in several sizes. Use those to plan your page layout. Move them around and choose the most appropriate sizes before actually stamping or gluing the page.

To Make the Page at Right

Here is a wonderful idea for including many small photographs on a single scrapbook page. Small, round adhesive-backed ink-jet printer stickers are stamped with a diploma image then colored with markers. The photographs are cut into circles and stuck to the backs of the diploma stickers. A sheet of cardstock has been covered with background stampings and embossing. Slots are cut into the cardstock page with a craft knife and the photo circles are inserted into them. A matte board spine is attached to the page's left edge so it can be inserted into a three-ring binder.

Every page begins with a layout. You may have a plan, a sketch, or even a template to follow when placing the various parts on a page. Or it may all occur by just moving the elements around on a blank background and choosing what looks best. The arrangement of those elements—photographs, words, colors, and decorative additions like stamped images—makes up the layout. As you study the artist pages throughout the book, think about the construction of the page, and try to see the basic layout that each artist used. Look for simplicity, balance, and use of color.

ARTIST: SUSAN JAWORSKI STRANC

Stamp an image onto plain, adhesive-backed stickers.

backgrounds

To Make the Page at Left

The background is created in two steps. First, stamp a sheet of pale, neutral cardstock with a large home decor fern stamp, randomly covering the page with two or three colors and leaving a faint impression. Use the medium lacy leaf stamp over the top of the fern layer, filling in some of the blank areas. Finally, stamp the small leaf multiple times on white cardstock with a heavier coat of the same colors. When dry, add letters to each stamping. Outline the letters with black pen and cut out the leaves. Place the words on the page, add a couple of blank leaf cutouts, and stamp a border along one edge of the page to balance the design.

Backgrounds

Combined with photographs or artwork, backgrounds are the most elemental part of a scrapbook page. They set the mood for the entire page, and act as a key to communicate the look and feel of all the elements and embellishments that will be added. In some cases, the background can stand alone, the only additions being the mechanics necessary for mounting or identifying the photographs. For example, look at the school background on page 26. Although the black letters stamped on red cardstock act as a border, they also create a background. The page elements in this case are self-explanatory, so the simple background is the only stamping required.

A variety of coordinating backgrounds may be stacked and layered to increase depth and interest on a page. This was done with blue, yellow, and orange in the sample shown on page 20. Stamping and embossing the entire background with dozens of small, patterned stampings, as in the birthday theme on page 22, is also effective.

Forever Yours: Double Wedding Pages

ARTIST: VICKI SCHREINER

To construct these coordinating wedding pages, stamp the roses and words with gold ink on white cardstock, then color the images with art pencils. Cut out the motifs and set aside. Make the frames on the left page by cutting squares, ovals, and rectangles, about ½" (1 cm) larger all around than the photos, from moss green cardstock. Trim the edges of the cardstock with paper edgers and adhere the photos, centered on top of the shapes. Make the large photo frame on the right page by cutting two corner triangles from the lace place mat and fitting them together to form a rectangle. Cut another smaller rectangle of handmade paper and center it on top of the lace one. Center the photograph on top of the handmade paper and add ribbon trim along each edge.

Place the framed photos on the striped pages, leaving room for ribbon garlands at the top of each page. Glue ribbon across the tops of the pages and add embellishments to the ribbon and to the frames.

MATERIALS

- **Stamps**
  Forever Yours
  Small rose engraving
  Romantic rose garland
  Romantic rose corner
- **Ink and Inkpads**
  Metallic gold ink
- **Papers**
  White cardstock
  Moss green cardstock
  White lace paper place mat
  Handmade paper
- **Miscellaneous**
  Art pencils
  Moss green acrylic paint, clear glaze base
  Removable tape
  Sponge
  Victorian paper edgers
  Ribbon

Step 1

Here is an easy and effective way to make a striped background. First, measure and lightly mark the top and bottom edge of the cardstock where the stripes will go. Place the cardstock on a large cardboard work surface, and lay the stripes with removable tape, extending them over the edge of the paper onto the cardboard. Sponge a thinned layer of paint and glaze base over the entire page, including the tape. Dip the sponge in the paint mixture and blot lightly on folded paper towels before applying to the page so the paint won't seep under the edges of the tape.

Step 2

Allow the paint to dry and carefully remove the tape to reveal the striped background. Repeat this background striping on as many pages as you need at one time so the colors on facing pages will match.

Step 3

Randomly stamp over the stripes with the rose stamp and gold ink, retaining a light and airy appearance. Ink the stamp and blot lightly on a folded paper towel to remove some of the ink. Experiment on a separate sheet of cardstock until you achieve the look you want, then re ink and stamp over the striped background.

The Queen Mary: Layered Background Page

ARTIST: SANDRA McCALL

Many stamp artists experiment with different stamps, inks, embossing methods, papers, and tools, then collect the resulting samples in a special box for later use. They also save scraps such as centers cut out of frames, strips trimmed from larger papers, and other bits and pieces produced during the creative process of making pages. If you set aside a regular time each week or each month for creative experimenting, you'll be surprised how quickly these beautiful examples will accumulate. You could also save scraps in page protectors and keep them in a 3-ring binder. Sort them by color, size, or theme and you'll always have a ready supply for embellishing your pages.

The background on this page only looks complicated to construct. It consists of three layers of stamped paper. Stamp the medium blue background paper with a linear patterned stamp and gold ink. For a border, skip the center of the page and stamp only a couple of inches (about 5 cm) around the edges of the dark blue cardstock.

Use the same stamp and ink to decorate about half a page of yellow cardstock to be used for corners and accents in the top layer.

To make the orange monoprint paper used for the middleground, follow the directions at right.

To Make a Monoprint

An interesting monoprint can be made with one of the following methods:

Method #1

Acrylic Paint: Mix three or four coordinating colors with retardant to slow the drying time, then pour them in puddles onto a sheet of flexible, clear vinyl or acetate to act as a transfer sheet. Daub here and there with a sponge to create interesting textures and slightly mix the colors, working quickly so the paint doesn't dry. Turn the sheet over onto a piece of cardstock or copy paper. With your hand, press down on the entire back surface of the transfer sheet to transfer the paint. For more interesting textures, press a rubber stamp onto the back of the transfer sheet, displacing some of the paint. Remove the sheet to expose the monoprint. You may be able to get two or three impressions before starting over, each one becoming progressively lighter in tone.

Method #2

Stamping Reinkers: Use inexpensive copy paper for its absorbency, and begin in the same way as for acrylic paint, squirting the reinkers directly onto the transfer sheet. Spread the ink by daubing with a sponge and turn the sheet over onto the copy paper. You will need more pressure to make the transfer, so press down on the transfer sheet with the wooden block of a rubber stamp, moving it over the entire sheet.

Birthday Boy: Embossed Background Page

This lively and cheerful background is perfect for portraying the mood and theme of a child's first birthday—it practically sings with joy and celebration.

To Make the Page at Left

To make the background, first use thinned acrylic paints or watercolors to paint a band of color at the top and the bottom of the background cardstock. Allow the paint to dry. Cut a mask of copy paper or cardstock the size and shape of the photograph and stick it to the center of the page with removable adhesive. Choose a square stamp with a small, allover pattern and cover the entire page, a little at a time, by stamping and embossing one area then moving on to the next. Be sure to stamp over the edges of the photo mask. When the page is covered, remove the mask. Mount the photo on a slightly larger block of cardstock and mount it in the masked-off area on the page. Stamp and emboss the letters and other elements separately, then cut them out and glue in place.

STAMPING TRICK

Plan ahead when making background paper and stamp an entire page (or several pages), even if you only need part of it for the page you are constructing. Put the extra pieces into your stash of scraps for later use.

Embossing Help

A tray with built-in funnel can be very helpful when embossing. Stamp the paper or cardstock with embossing ink, then place it in the tray and liberally pour on the embossing powder. Pick up the paper, holding it over the tray, and tap the excess powder into the tray, then use the funnel to pour the powder back into its original container. Wipe off the inside of the tray and put the paper back in while you use the heat tool to emboss the piece. For 8 ½" × 11" (22 cm × 28 cm) sheets, choose the larger tray.

To Make the Page at Left

Choose a bright turquoise cardstock and stamp the border all around with a giraffe stamp and bronze or gold metallic ink. Using the same ink, fill the center of the page with repetitions of a tiger stamp. With black pigment ink, cover the entire surface with the largest pattern on a crackle cube stamp. Randomly stamp a black leaf image over the page to fill in empty spaces. Stamp letters on gold foil with black embossing ink and dry with a heat tool. Cut out the individual letters with paper edgers and glue in place. This treatment could be used to add color and depth to any page.

STAMPING TRICK

To make a straight, clean inside edge on a border around an entire 8 1/2" × 11" (22 cm × 28 cm) page, cut out a rectangle of copy paper or cardstock 2" (5 cm) smaller all around, which would be 4 1/2" × 7" (11 cm × 18 cm). Center this mask on the page with temporary adhesive, then stamp the border. Remove the mask to reveal a border with a sharp, clean edge.

Borders

There is a very fine line between what is considered a border and what is considered a frame, and sometimes it's impossible to separate the two. When referring to a border, we usually think of a design that goes around all the edges of the page. Although a border may frame a page, the term "frame" is most often used for a design that surrounds an individual element on the page.

A border gives a scrapbook page a more finished look and increases the beauty and elegance of photographs and other elements that it surrounds.

For the page shown at left, a wide, even border was stamped on the page before any other elements were added. You could also place photos first and add a border that overlaps some of them and ties the elements together. An example of this method is shown in the portraits of Friends on page 30. A border may be repeated stampings of the same image, or it may include several different images. Try different stamps in different, coordinating colors, and try several different stamps in the same color.

Stamp a pale background cardstock with slightly darker neutral color ink and fill in the open areas with watercolor pencils that match the photographs and other images on the page. This technique can create effective and beautiful borders as in the decorative flower borders at the top and bottom of the twin babies photograph on page 83. This artful border could also be used all around a page to enhance photos or other artwork.

Today is Friday: Simple Stamped Border

This is a wonderful and simple way to display a child's school papers. The page is clear and direct, enhances the subject, and is very easy to duplicate. If you have a good photo of the child as well as a school assignment, you have the basic elements for creating this treasure.

ARTIST: pj DUTTON

QUICK TRICK

Tie page elements together by framing them all with the same thin border in black or a color. Angle some of the elements on the page instead of lining everything up in straight rows.

MATERIALS

- **Stamps**
  Block letters
  Block numbers
- **Ink and Inkpads**
  Black pigment
- **Paper**
  Black cardstock
  Red cardstock
- **Miscellaneous**
  Black photo corners

To Make the Page

Cut a piece of black cardstock about a ¼" (5 mm) larger on all sides than the photo and mount the photo to it. Repeat for the school paper, rounding the corners of the cardstock. Trim ¼" (5 mm) off the edges of the red cardstock, round the corners, and stamp the border around the sheet. Mount the red cardstock to a sheet of black. Move the items around until you are satisfied with the arrangement, then glue the school paper to the background and mount the photo with black photo corners.

Wanda and Ferd Jr: A Heritage Children's Page

ARTIST: pj DUTTON

This subtle border recedes into the background, adding importance to the photo, thereby accentuating the expressions on the faces of the children. Borders may be bright and colorful or simple and elegant. They may also be very subtle, adding just enough color and pattern to set off the page elements and give the illusion of depth at the edges of the page.

MATERIALS

- **Stamps**
  Fancy flourish Bollio
  Tag block
- **Ink and Inkpads**
  Eggshell white and black pigment inks
  Metallic bronze embossing powder
- **Paper**
  Black cardstock
  White cardstock
- **Miscellaneous**
  Eggshell or cream marker
  Gold pen

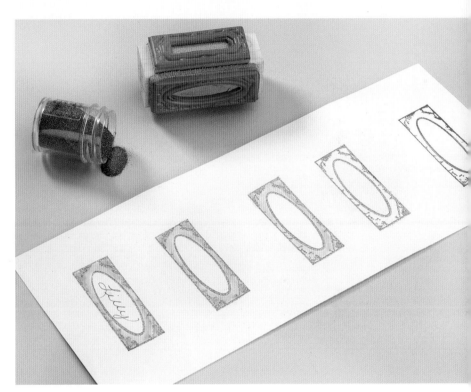

Getting Started

To create this subtle border, use pigment ink that almost disappears when you stamp it on the black cardstock. A Bollio stamp looks like a long wooden rolling pin with its sides squared off and long, narrow stamps adhered to each side. (See page 75 for an example of a Bolio stamp.) Because the stamp is about 10" (25 cm) long, it will cover almost the entire length of an 8½" × 11" (22 cm × 28 cm) page in one step. Place the Bollio on the work surface with the stamping side you have selected facing up. Ink the entire length of the long, narrow stamp by patting it repeatedly with an inkpad. Place the edge of the sheet of black cardstock face down on the inked stamp. Press the back of the sheet with your fingertips, all along the surface of the stamp, to transfer the image onto the edge of the page.

Adding the Photo

The frame for this photograph is made with a block stamp which is applied to the center of the page, creating a solid block of color with a ragged edge. The photo is printed a little smaller than the block and then mounted on top of it so the edges form a frame. The block stamp is shown on page 35.

Making the Labels

Stamp the labels for the photos with black ink on white cardstock and emboss with bronze powder. Let dry, color the frames with markers, and write the names with a gold pen. Cut out and attach to the black page.

Friends: Layered Border Pages

ARTIST: SANDRA McCALL

This bright and imaginative border combines several techniques and unifies the page with careful placement of all the elements. At first glance, it seems not to be a border at all. Some of the photos are repeated on the right page in a smaller format, and they form part of the border.

QUICK TRICK

When creating or ordering the photographs for a page, get several copies of the featured photos in small prints, about 1" × 2" (3 cm × 5 cm), depending on the shape of the original. Cut out the smaller photos and repeat them to form a border.

Getting Started

To make a page like those shown at the left, stamp and decorate many sheets of paper and cardstock in a variety of bright colors and patterns. Choose patterns that will look good when cut into strips or other small shapes. Stamp some sheets with allover patterns of the same motifs in a larger size. Coordinate the colors, but don't let them clash or become too repetitive. The technique for making beautiful Faux Batik paper may be found in the Basics section of the book (page 11).

Arranging the Page

Once you have created several sheets of coordinated paper, gather your photos and begin laying all the elements on a sheet of blank cardstock. Look for designs that will complement the features of the photos, and carry out the theme of the page. This one is joyful and light, so the colors accent that feeling of happy and carefree times. The colors and shapes harmonize with the mood of the page but do not fight with the photos for prominence.

Using Photos in a Border

Repeating the photo on the lower portion of the right page creates an illusion of depth, so the larger image almost steps out of the border with lighthearted movement.

To Make the Page at Left

Ink a solid block frame stamp with a sponge, leaving the center of the stamp free of ink. Randomly stamp with several colors over the entire page, cleaning the stamp between colors. Use a smaller frame stamp to fill in some of the blank areas, then stamp the small frame several times on some coordinating parchment stock and emboss in gold. After the embossing has set, add colored pencil in the center of each stamped frame for contrast. Next, stamp the letters with pigment ink inside each frame. Cut out the framed letters and apply to the background with paper glue. Finally, trim the edges of the background paper with paper edgers and glue the entire layout to a sheet of contrasting cardstock. This method can be used successfully with photographs or artwork by simply changing the number of frames and using different letters.

Frames

Creating just the right frame to complement treasured artwork and photographs can be both rewarding and enjoyable. Frames can add just the right mood to a photograph or piece of art, and they can focus attention on the area of a page you wish to highlight. They can be subtle decorations or pronounced design elements. A frame can be created as a separate element that is added to the page, giving it dimension and texture. This chapter contains a variety of ideas for creating unique frames for scrapbook pages.

Simple frames may be stamped around a photograph to contrast or coordinate with the background paper. To create this look, stamp the background first, then trim the photograph and glue it on top of the stamped frame to preserve a clean edge. This method is used on the frames around Ferdinand and Lilly in their 1894 portraits shown on page 34.

Ferdinand and Lily: A Heritage Page

The ink used here is platinum, and it takes on a colorful patina when stamped on black cardstock. Try stamping in different colors on various papers to discover what works best with the photograph or artwork you wish to frame.

This is a companion page to Wanda and Ferd Jr. on page 28, but each can stand alone.

STAMPING TRICK

Stamp the frame with a bright, vibrant color of pigment ink, and apply the photograph separately to a layer of white cardstock. Cut out the photo and glue it over the stamping to preserve the clarity and contrast.

- **Stamps**
  Color block
  Tag block
  Fancy flourish Bollio
- **Ink and Inkpads**
  Eggshell white, platinum, and black pigment
  Metallic bronze embossing powder
- **Papers**
  White cardstock
  White cardstock
  White paper
- **Miscellaneous**
  Markers
  Metallic pen

Getting Started

To make this very simple page, stamp a border around the edges of a sheet of black cardstock using a flourish Bollio and eggshell white pigment ink, although platinum might be interesting for variety. Stamp three platinum or eggshell frames directly onto the page, allowing space for nameplates at the top and bottom. The two upper photos were stamped with a smaller frame stamp than the single one below them. Size the photos to fit into the stamped frames, and mount them on white paper before placing them on top of the stamping.

Adding the Names

To make the nameplates, first stamp the images with embossing ink on white cardstock, then emboss them and write the names with a metallic pen. Cut them out and place them above or below the appropriate photographs.

The frame stamp is composed of a background block with a built-in frame around it. It can be stamped with pigment ink, as on this page, or with dye ink, markers, or embossing ink and powder. Each treatment will produce a very different look and mood.

ARTIST: DAWN HOUSER

Mothers and Daughters:
Stamped Family Pages

A frame doesn't have to be four-sided to be effective. Stamp a crown or other image and attach on only two sides of a photograph, as shown here on the photo of the grandmother with her granddaughter. This design adds just enough elegance to convey the heritage quality of the photograph—any more embellishment would detract from the face.

Frames needn't be conventional in shape. The dress form image acts as a frame when the photographs are cut out in its shape and no other frame is applied, anchoring the photo to the page. To create a unique photo edge, first stamp a shape such as the dress form on thin white or tracing paper and cut it out. Lay it over the chosen photograph and pencil around the shape, then trim the photo. Here, a montage of several photographs is used to make an image large enough to fit the dress form. This treatment adds interest and character to the entire page and could be used to accentuate a particular theme by using the appropriate icons.

Flower Babies: Accents as Frames

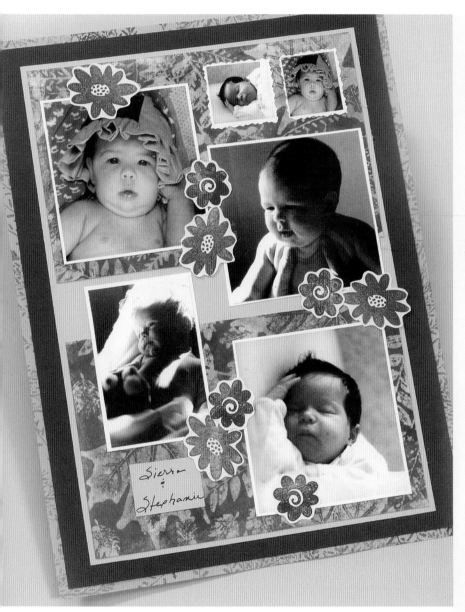

You can embellish a frame by adding one or more paper appliqués. Here, single and multiple images are stamped on a separate sheet of paper, then cut out and glued partially over the edge of the photographs and the background. The pink and fuchsia flowers surrounding the sweet faces enhance these adorable baby photos.

This method allows the freedom to experiment with colors and shapes before committing to a particular design. You can stamp many flowers, hearts, stars and other shapes on white paper, cut them out, then sprinkle them on the pages of your scrapbook, only gluing down the ones you like.

MATERIALS

- **Stamps**

  Small flowers

  Large oak leaf, leaf spray and fern

- **Ink and ink pads**

  Small petal shaped and Cat's Eye pigment ink pads

  Magenta to green dye inks

- **Papers**

  One sheet plum cardstock

  Two sheets white cardstock

  One or two sheets pale yellow paper

  Two or three sheets white copy paper

- **Miscellaneous**

  Scissors

  Household bleach

  Paper towels

  Large nylon paint brush or brayer

QUICK TRICK

When making copies of your photographs, print several different sizes, including some as small as postage stamps, so you can arrange them in a variety of ways before affixing them to the page. Repeating the same image in several sizes can be used to focus the eye where you want it to go for maximum impact.

Getting Started

Step 1

Protect your work surface and wear old clothing since you'll be using bleach. Start with a sheet of light colored cardstock. You could also try a matte copier paper or art paper.

Step 2

Press the small pigment ink pads directly on the paper, alternating and turning them as you work to swirl the colors all over the page. Rub the colors into the paper with paper towels.

Step 3

Paint or brayer dark magenta to green dye ink over the surface, covering the pigment ink.

Step 4

Pour the bleach into several layers of folded paper towels in a dish and pat the stamps on the bleach as you would use an ink pad. Stamp off most of the dye ink, revealing the leaf patterns in pigment ink underneath. The bleach will lighten as it dries, and you can speed the process with a hair dryer or heat tool. Rinse stamps immediately in cool running water and dry them.

Making the Flowers

Stamp the flower images on white cardstock using dye ink, and cut them out leaving small white margins around them so they will stand out from the page.

Finishing the Page

Up to seven layers of paper are used in some areas of this precious scrapbook page. Layer successively smaller sheets of plum, yellow, and faux batik papers. Mount the photographs in various sizes on white cardstock and cut them out with a narrow white margin. Place the photographs on the background and sprinkle flowers around the page to tie it all together. Make the labels from pale yellow cardstock.

My Sister's Wedding: Embellished Pages

ARTIST: SANDRA McCALL

Materials such as beads, ribbons, paper lace, and wire can be applied over a stamping to create a frame that is a work of art. The significance and joy expressed in the wedding photographs deserve the attention and the extra time and care that these techniques require. For this design, stamp and emboss the background paper, then separately stamp and emboss pieces of cardstock to surround the photographs.

- **Stamps**
  Swirl stamp
  Assorted small image stamps
  Large heart with bow
  Bouquet
- **Ink and Inkpads**
  Gold metal extra and cream white pigment
  Pearl embossing powder
- **Paper**
  Mocha cardstock
  White cardstock
  Cream cardstock
- **Miscellaneous**
  Brush markers
  Two-way glue pen
  Gold dimensional fabric paint
  Beads, gold cording, pieces of dress lace, various trims

Getting Started

Use swirl stamps and metallic ink to decorate both the bottom and middle layers of these pages. Using metallic ink instead of embossing the designs will create an even surface under the photos, and they will lie flat on the page.

Cut several rectangles of the decorated papers in a variety of sizes. Make a pleasing arrangement on the mocha cardstock and glue them down, or choose a single rectangle to mount at the center of each page.

Mounting the Photos

Print the photos you wish to use for this page, including some small versions of several images. Mount each photo on white cardstock and cut them all out, leaving a ¼" (5 mm) margin around each one. Arrange them on the page, moving them around to find the best layout, then glue them in place.

Making the Photo Frames

Stamp some frames on mocha cardstock using gold metallic ink, cut out and form into strips by cutting apart at the corners. Apply around the photographs. Glue strings of beads around the larger photos, just at the edge of the images. Add gold cording around the rows of beads to embellish the frames.

QUICK TRICK

When applying lace, beads, and other embellishments to a page, apply glue to the page with a glue pen, then pick up the trim between a thin-bladed craft knife and your forefinger and use the knife for precise placement. Press the trim into the glue.

ARTIST: SANDRA McCALL

Add More Embellishments

Stamp bouquets, hearts, and other images on white cardstock, embossing as desired, and color with markers. Cut out and place among the other elements on the pages for emphasis. Tie a sheer narrow bow or add some lace from the wedding gown for a personal touch.

To Make the Page at Left

Stamp the background with a large flower block and then a smaller leaf stamp using multicolored ink. With paper edgers, trim about 1/2" (1 cm) from all four sides of the page and save the trimmed pieces. Mount the entire page on a sheet of contrasting cardstock. To make a perfectly square corner, stamp and emboss a flourish on the lower right corner of an uncut vellum sheet. Use paper edgers to trim it into a rounded fan shape. With a glue stick and a narrow line of glue, adhere only the straight edges of the vellum to the edges of the background. Vellum wrinkles easily when liquid glue is applied, so a glue stick is a good choice. Glue a thin strip of the reserved background piece over the glue line on the vellum corner to hide any wrinkles. Cut another piece of vellum into a fan shape, stamp the word on it, trim the upper curve with paper edgers, then tuck it into the corner pocket.

STAMPING TRICK

Sort through your stash of leftover and experimental stamped paper to find the colors and patterns that work with the page you are constructing. Cut two perfect squares about 1" – 2" (3 cm – 5 cm) across then cut them into triangles to make four matching corners.

ARTIST: BETTY AUTH

Corners

Corners for scrapbooks originated as a handy way to hold photos on a page. Our grandmothers only saw them in black, with gummy backs that had to be moistened. Today's corners still act as photo anchors, but their looks have expanded to include pure decoration and fanciful creativity. On page 68, you will see clocks and keys that are stamped, cut out and used as corners. Another example of corners is found on page 76—the corner has been cut directly into the background. Almost any stamp with a fairly solid shape can be turned into a corner, and there are examples for you to discover throughout this book.

Snow Day: Corners Made with Stamps

Corners and embellishment for the large photo at the bottom of this wintry scene are made with a combination of techniques, all easy to do. The snowflakes clustered around the photographs add to the crisp, cold feeling of the snow scenes, enhancing the frosty mood of the page.

ARTIST: SANDRA McCALL

Making the Corners

Step 1
On a piece of blue cardstock, pencil in a dot where each corner of the trimmed large photo will be. Stamp and emboss a white snowflake over each dot.

Step 2
Cluster more embossed snowflakes around the first one, allowing some to overlap the rectangle where the photograph will go. Cut around the inside edge of the snowflakes at each corner of the stamping and slip the trimmed photograph corners through the slits.

Step 3
The corners of the photo actually slide through to the back of the blue cardstock, holding it in place. Finally, trim around the entire assemblage and adhere it to the page.

MATERIALS

- **Stamps**
  Snowflakes
  Tiny snowflakes
  Background block
- **Ink and Inkpads**
  White pigment
  White embossing powder
- **Papers**
  Paper for faux batik or decorative paper
  Blue cardstock

Getting Started

Size the photos so they fit on the blue cardstock page and leave plenty of room for the snowflake accents and corners. Trim the photographs with deckle paper edgers, leaving some of the white margin around each one. Make the faux batik middle ground paper using the technique on page 11 of the Basics chapter or on page 37, or select a sheet of decorative paper and cut a piece about half the size of an 8 ½" × 11" (22 cm × 28 cm) page. Stamp a sheet of blue cardstock with the tiny snowflake background block and white pigment ink. Set these aside while making the corners.

STAMPING TRICKS

Begin with a selection of photographs that convey the spirit of friends enjoying a good time together in a wintry scene, or choose several frosty white views of a pristine, snowy land-scape. Add blue paper and white, embossed snowflakes to increase the chilly atmosphere.

Emboss the most important elements on a page so they will stand out, and stamp, without embossing, coordinating images on the rest of the page in the same color. This will create a unified look and highlight the areas you wish to emphasize.

National Clown Week: Elemental Corners

ARTIST: pj DUTTON

There are no rules that dictate the shape of a corner. Advanced printing techniques for photographs have made it affordable to obtain many copies or photo prints at home or at the copy store, so you can experiment with copies while valuable originals are safely tucked away. You can feel free to create diverse, exuberant stamped scrapbook pages like these!

MATERIALS

- **Stamps**
  Cube with four simple elements
  Harlequin scrap
  Small alphabet
- **Ink and Inkpads**
  Saffron, indigo, pine, cardinal, and coal pigment
- **Papers**
  Three or four sheets each of white, black, and dark blue cardstock
- **Miscellaneous**
  Square and large circle cutters (optional)
  Circle punches, 1/2", 1", 1 1/2" (1 cm, 3 cm, 4 cm) (optional)

Step 1

Mount the larger photographs on colored cardstock and trim to about a 1/2" (1 cm) border all around. Place the photos on a piece of white cardstock but don't glue down. Make a light pencil mark on the cardstock at each corner of each photo to mark where it will go, then remove the photos.

Step 2

Use four colors of ink and a cube with four coordinating stamps to stamp directly over the pencil marks, centering each of them on the marks.

Step 3

Erase the pencil marks and use a craft knife to cut along the inside edge of each stamping, creating corners into which the photo can be inserted.

Step 4

Cut out the assemblage and mount it on the page. As an option, stamp the corners separately on white cardstock and cut each of them out. Cut around the inside lines of the swirls and the squiggles using a craft knife. Layer them over the corners of the mounted photos on the scrapbook page.

To Make the Small Round Photos

Punch or cut out the small face photo circles and punch or cut out black cardstock circles just a little larger than the photos. Mount the photos on the black circles before mounting them on the page.

To Finish the Page

With the harlequin stamp and coal ink, randomly decorate the border of a sheet of white cardstock, keeping in mind the placement of the photographs. Stamp the letters individually on white cardstock, cut them into squares and decorate the edges of each square. Punch or cut some smaller circles from black cardstock and glue the letters on them. Mount the words across the two pages, continuing from one to the other. Trim 1/2" (1 cm) off each side of the white cardstock and mount the entire page on a sheet of dark blue cardstock.

Garden Beauties: Folded Origami Corners

These gorgeous pages incorporate origami folding into the construction of the corners. The artist is an avid gardener, and has made dramatic pages to enclose some of her most stunning blooms. Why not make art scrapbooks to display photos of your own favorite hobbies? Change the papers and colors to suit a number of themes from model airplanes to butterfly collections.

To practice origami, begin with a 4" × 4" (10 cm × 10 cm) or a 6" × 6" (15 cm × 15 cm) square of paper. Once you have perfected the technique, move down to a 2" × 2" (5 cm × 5 cm) square for the actual corners.

ARTIST: SUSAN JAWORSKI STRANC

STAMPING TRICK

Origami papers are often very shiny, but the metallics are dazzling when they are stamped and embossed. Use a large, open stamped image so the folding won't interfere with the details in the embossing and cause it to crack.

Folding the Corners

Fold a square as you read the steps, always looking one or two steps ahead. Dashed lines indicate folds.

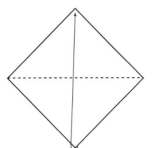

Step 1
Lay a square of origami paper diagonally on the work surface, right side down, and fold the lower point up to form a triangle.

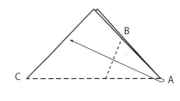

Step 2
With the folded edge at the bottom, fold point A to the center of the left side of the triangle, making the top of the folded corner parallel to the base of the triangle.

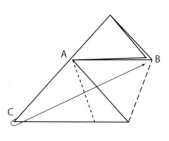

Step 3
Fold point C to point B.

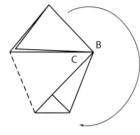
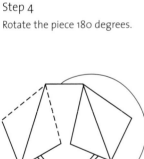

Step 4
Rotate the piece 180 degrees.

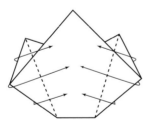

Step 5
Unfold the right corner.

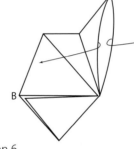

Step 6
Slip your finger inside the corner to open it.

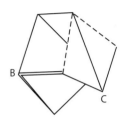

Step 7
Flatten the corner, aligning the front and back creases. Unfold the left corner and repeat steps 6 and 7.

Step 8
Rotate the piece 180 degrees and turn it over.

Step 9
Fold both corners in toward the center, following the original crease lines.

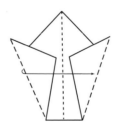

Step 10
Fold the piece in half from left to right.

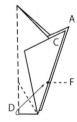

Step 11
To make creases in the base, fold the bottom of the piece up, matching point D to point F.

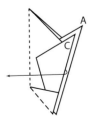

Step 12
Unfold the base and open the piece back to the way it was in Step 10.

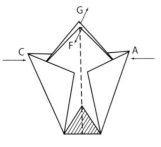

Step 13
Insert a finger into the center of the piece to open it.

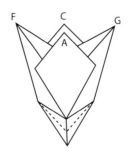

Step 14
Make a half turn from left to right and push the triangular base section up inside the piece.

Step 15
The finished piece, ready to accept the corner of your artwork or photo.

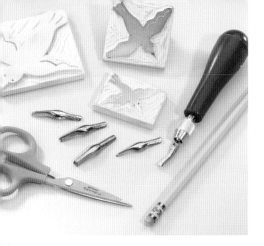

To Make the Page at Left

Make cutout shapes that act like die cuts by carving three sizes of simple bird shapes from stamp carving blocks. Lightly draw the designs onto the carving block with a lead pencil or draw them on paper, cut them out, and trace around the paper shapes onto the block. Keeping the design minimal, carve around the bird and add just a few details. For the background, choose bright blue cardstock and a purple, pink, and green rainbow inkpad. Using the purple range of the pad, stamp the smallest birds heading toward the upper left corner of the paper. Use the green and pink color range to stamp the medium birds heading toward the upper right corner. Stamp the largest birds with opaque white, some heading left and some right. Use all the colors to stamp two large birds on dark blue cardstock and cut them out. Stamp letters on yellow cardstock and cut them out, then make a yellow banner and decorate the folds with sepia chalk. Glue the letters to the banner, the banner to the background, and the two large birds as if they're holding the corners of the banner. Trim the background with paper edgers and mount on yellow cardstock.

Die Cuts

Traditional die cuts for scrapbooking are machine-cut paper shapes available at arts and crafts or scrapbooking stores. They come in a variety of colors and themes, and may be purchased singly or in packets. There are many ways to combine cutout shapes with stamps, and you will see them scattered throughout this book. For a quick and simple addition, decorate purchased shapes with stamps to match your other artwork, as shown on page 51. To add interest and dimension to a scrapbook page, stamp an image and then cut it out completely or partially to create your own faux die cut shape. A beautiful example of this technique is shown in the intricate booklet on page 54.

STAMPING TRICK

Add personal flair to your pages by carving your own stamps. It's sometimes difficult to find the exact image you want for a given situation, so express your sentiments by making the stamps yourself. See the Basics section, page 12, for instructions.

Fall Foliage: Decorated Die Cuts

To use different cutout shapes on the same page without having them clash, tie the theme and the elements together by stamping on the cutouts and also on the background paper. Then use art pencils to blend all the pieces together.

ARTIST: VICKI SCHREINER

Colors can be used to pull together various elements on a scrapbook page. If the pieces of a layout seem to clash, try using art or oil pencils and touches of the same colors over the entire page to help coordinate them.

MATERIALS

• **Stamps**
  Tiny cluster of ivy
  Fall leaf

• **Ink and Inkpads**
  Khaki, bamboo, and bronze pigment inkpads

• **Paper**
  Dark olive cardstock
  Barn wood, plaid, and white papers

• **Miscellaneous**
  Fall leaf and acorn die cuts
  Oil color pencils
  White plastic eraser (to erase the oil color pencils if needed)

Getting Started

These acorns and leaves are part of a seasonal packet containing a variety of colors and shapes. While they are pleasing, and the basic colors are appropriate for the fall scrapbook theme on page 50, they need some additional embellishment to blend with the page.

Making the Border

Stamp the fall leaf around the edge of the barn wood paper, turning the stamp for each impression, and color softly with oil pencils.

Making the Frames

Use a craft knife to cut along the lines of the plaid paper to make frames for each photo, lightly glue them around the photos, then mount the framed photos on slightly larger pieces of dark olive cardstock. Glue the photo assemblages to the background page and scatter the acorn and leaf cutouts over the page, letting some overlap the edges of the frames.

Stamp the red leaves with the leaf stamp and bamboo ink. Stamp the lower part of the acorns with the tiny ivy pattern and bronze ink. Let dry and use oil pencils to lightly color the leaves on the acorn, covering the rest of the shape with a white paper mask to protect from smudges as you work. Add pencil shading to the bodies of the acorns to emphasize the caps.

Summertime Fun: Cut Outs and Die Cuts

ARTIST: DAWN HOUSER

Two different die cut ideas are shown on this page. The red shapes at the bottom of the page resemble summertime surfboards and help carry out the theme of the page. The green Hawaiian-style shirt is made from a stamp and it has been cut along one side to lay over the edge of the photograph. The inside of the shirt is covered with a piece of turquoise paper, cut to fit, and glued in place.

No photo on this page has its borders completely intact. Interrupt the regularity and sameness of rectangular shapes by overlapping with die cuts and by angling the photos to extend beyond the edges of the page.

QUICK TRICK

Place part of a handmade or purchased die cut over the edge of a photograph to accent the photo or to hide an unwanted element within it.

Another Way to Use Cut Outs

Create a cutout shape from a bow or other stamped image, then select a portion of the cutout to lap over the edge of the photograph. This works best if you choose a stamp composed of solid shapes and stamp it on cardstock.

If using a bow, try placing one streamer over the corner of a photo, or use the entire bow at the top or bottom of the photo. Placement of any cutout will depend on the arrangement of all the elements on the page, and on the subject within the photo.

ARTIST: BETTY AUTH

A Sailing Trip: Pop-up Cut Outs

Die cuts and cutouts can change the pages of a scrapbook from flat to fabulous. In this case, the artist used a single sailboat stamp as the inspiration for a faux booklet. For the reader, it's an adventure of discovery as each new page is lifted and the sailing trip is revealed.

ARTIST: SUSAN JAWORSKI STRANC

QUICK TRICK

To produce sharp cutouts, use a new knife blade each time you start a page. Blades are inexpensive, and should be changed often. Work on a self-healing cutting mat with a standard or swivel knife and turn the paper as you go. Use medium-weight cardstock or art paper and test it with the knife before starting a complicated page. Be patient.

MATERIALS

- **Stamps**
  Small sailboat
- **Ink and Inkpads**
  Medium blue pigment
- **Paper**
  Blue charcoal art paper
- **Miscellaneous**
  Craft knife with extra blades
  Cutting mat

Step 1

Draw a wavy pencil line across the paper for a guide. Stamp the sailboat several times along the wavy line with the hull on the line. Use blue ink that is just dark enough to see, but not dark enough to show after the page is complete. Some of the papers are turned to the front and some to the back when the sailboats move across the page to the left. Stamp so the sails are barely touching one another.

Step 2

With the craft knife, cut out the areas between the sailboats across the paper. This will help hold the row together when cutting small parts.

Step 3

Cut out the sails and the rest of the outline, leaving the joins between the sails intact so the page does not fall apart. As the pages of the booklet are opened, more photographs of the sailing trip are revealed.

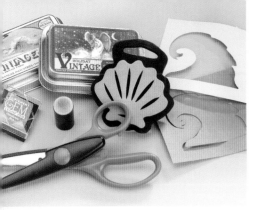

To Create the Page at Left

Start with a sheet of white cardstock, a shell home decor stamp, some wave cutouts, and a variety of blue, turquoise, and sea foam green pigment inks. You'll also need a sponge dauber, white pigment ink, and some paper edgers in a wave pattern. Stamp the shells over the white cardstock, varying the colors of ink. With the wave edgers, trim the stamped page to 6" × 9 " (15 cm × 23 cm), saving the strips. With light blue ink, stamp four shells on a second sheet of white cardstock and cut them out. Arrange three of the shells in a banner, glue lightly together, and stamp the letters on them. Embellish the waves with white pigment ink and a dauber sponge. Assemble the page, layering the 6" × 9" (15 cm × 23 cm) stamped paper slightly left of center on a sheet of blue cardstock. Trim some of the reserved strips and align them vertically and horizontally near the top and right edges of the blue cardstock. Daub some color on the fourth shell and glue it over the strips at the upper right. Glue the waves in place, then daub a bit of dark blue ink on the curl of each wave, along the base of the word banner, and around the base of the upper right shell.

ARTIST: BETTY AUTH

Stickers

The aisles of craft and scrapbooking stores are filled with wonderful stickers to use on your pages, and occasionally these purchased stickers are just what you need. But sometimes you want stickers that are special, and will highlight your photos in a particular way. When this is the case, make your own stickers with stamps. If you have a laminating machine with sticker-making capabilities, you can run your stampings through it to create stickers. If you don't have a machine, you can usually take your stamped images to a scrapbooking store and have them turned into stickers.

QUICK TRICK

To create a foamy, frothy appearance on the tops of the waves, use a dauber and white pigment ink before you push the shapes out of the background, and lightly daub the white ink along the tops of the waves. When they are pushed out, the lines will be crisp and the foam will fade in toward the body of the waves.

School Days and Birthdays: Sticker Pages

ARTIST: VICKI SCHREINER

These two pages illustrate the variety of looks and themes you can achieve with the addition of handmade stickers. The page at the left features ice cream cones that make a statement because of their size. Two stamps were combined to create the cute little ducks floating down on bunches of balloons.

On the right page, stamps with a school theme perk up the page and help balance the strong colors and lettering used throughout.

MATERIALS FOR BIRTHDAY PAGE

- Stamps

  Assorted small to medium stamps
- Ink and Inkpads

  Pinecone and baby blue pigment

  Clear embossing ink and sparkle powder
- Papers

  One sheet each of periwinkle dots, periwinkle strings, solid periwinkle

  One sheet light yellow cardstock

  Two sheets white cardstock
- Miscellaneous

  Laminating machine with sticker-making capabilities

  Pastel alphabet stickers

  Embossing tool

  Victorian paper edgers

  Assorted markers

MATERIALS FOR SCHOOL DAYS PAGE

- Stamps

  Assorted school stamps
- Ink and Inkpads

  Black pigment inkpad
- Papers

  One sheet alphabet paper

  One sheet each red, green, and yellow corrugated

  One sheet each red and green cardstock

  Two sheets white cardstock
- Miscellaneous

  Laminating machine with sticker-making capabilities

  Easel die cut

  Assorted markers

  Removable tape

Making the Pages

These two pages are made in a similar way. Stamp the images onto white cardstock, emboss with sparkle powder for the birthday page, and stamp with black pigment ink for the school page. Color the images with markers and cut them out.

Run the cutouts through a laminating/sticker-making machine and set aside. Construct the pages, leaving plenty of white space, and add the stickers.

STAMPING TRICKS

When making your own stickers, stamp more images than you will need. Color with markers and choose only the best ones to convert into stickers. This will free your creativity and encourage you to experiment with the materials. In most cases, the stickers will look best on the page if they overlap the edges of the photos or other elements. The little floating ducks on the birthday page are an exception because they are used as space fillers while also adding accents and whimsy to the page. On the school page, some of the stickers are placed in an overlapping position while others are not. Notice how the school buses touch and slightly overlap the schoolhouse to provide unity and create a border. More school buses could be added in front of and behind the two shown, lengthening the border.

Buddy and Friends: Repeating Borders

ARTIST: SANDRA McCALL

The border along the bottom of these pages is made up of several small versions of the cat photo shown elsewhere. The cat has been cut out and applied over the top of a checkerboard strip. This is a very effective treatment because it harmonizes with the other elements, adds depth, and emphasizes the importance of the precious cat.

Notice how the narrow checkerboard carries across from one page to the other, tying them together and repeating the colors and patterns.

- **Stamps**
  Two or three small flowers
  Background swirls
  Checkerboard border
  Saying with heart flowers
- **Ink and Inkpads**
  White, yellow, and black pigment pads
  Rainbow dye inkpad
  Blue and magenta dye inks
- **Papers**
  Two sheets of black cardstock
  Monoprinted or handmade paper for middle ground
  Two sheets of 20# all-purpose copy paper
- **Miscellaneous**
  Variety of markers
  Deckle paper edgers
  White or silver gel pen

STAMPING TRICK

When stamping, save all your scraps and small bits to use later. The bright flowers seen on these two pages are also used in a very different context with the babies on page 36. When you find an image you like, stamp extras and use them throughout your scrapbook pages.

Getting Started

Before beginning to assemble this page, make several color copies of the photographs. Vary the sizes of the photos, and use deckle paper edgers to trim some of them. You will need about ten stamp-sized copies of one photo for the lower border. Choose a small version of one of the photographs used elsewhere on the page.

Making the Background

Use white pigment ink to stamp the swirl pattern over the two sheets of black cardstock for the background. Make two sheets of monoprint paper as described in The Basics section, page 11, or select two coordinating sheets of handmade paper. Make the checkerboard strips by stamping several rows of checks on white copy paper. Rub some yellow pigment ink over the checkers, then spot-color them with markers to coordinate with the monoprint paper. Stamp fifteen to eighteen flowers on copy paper with dye inks and cut them out.

Lay the two black background sheets next to one another on the work surface. Trim two pieces of monoprint or handmade paper to cover about two-thirds of each page and mount them similarly on each black page. Mount a strip of checkerboard across the bottoms of the pages, ½" (1 cm) up from the bottom, and make sure they are even. Cut out eight or more small photos and place them on top of the checkerboard strip, spacing evenly on each page.

Adding the Photos

Mount the remaining photos on the two pages, over the background and the middle ground. Use the largest photos or the featured photos on the left page, and the smaller ones on the right. Cut more strips of checkerboard and make frames and lines from the left page to the right page, continuing them at an angle across the two pages to tie the composition together. Cut out the small flowers and scatter them over the pages along with the stamped saying. Write some labels on black cardstock and cut them out to make the title blocks, then mount them on the pages.

Pet Memorial: Multi-page Booklet

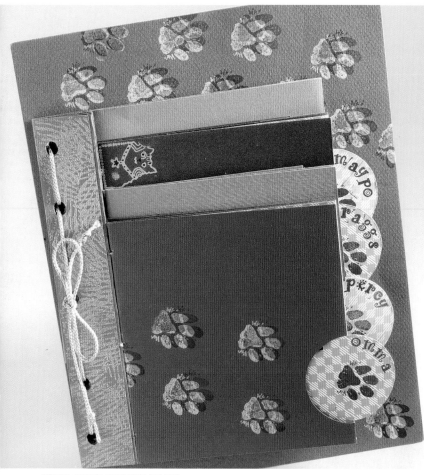

ARTIST: SUSAN JAWORSKI STRANC

Although the artist stamped the paw prints directly on the tabs in constructing this booklet, stickers would be an ideal way to avoid risking a misplaced stamp after a page is created. Simply stamp the images and write the names and years on individual round shapes, make them into stickers, and affix them to the pages.

When this booklet page is closed, all the tabs are visible. It is composed of four photo pages, each dedicated to a different pet who shared the lives of the artist and her family at various times. To add more pages, make the spine longer; to subtract pages, make it shorter.

Each page of the booklet is constructed separately with cardstock and art paper joined together, creating a sturdy, double-thick page.

Making the Pages

The small purple pages at right seem very different from the pet pages to the left, but their construction is the same. This technique would make a great journal of the garden, or a terrific recipe book. To make the pages, begin with a rectangle of purple cardstock and a smaller rectangle of green cardstock or paper. The smaller piece should be about one-third the size of the larger one. Glue the green piece flush with one edge of the purple paper and offset slightly from center. To make the pointed tab, use a template to lightly pencil a diamond shape on the green rectangle, positioning it about ½" (1 cm) from the edge. Mark a line across the green strip exactly at the center of the diamond and use the craft knife to cut out the half of the circle that is nearest the edge. Fold the page on the line that bisects the diamond so the cut end sticks up and the cardstock is folded back against itself. Glue the folded part in place and weigh it down with a book until dry, creating a tab. Use a veggie stamp to make a sticker from a separate piece of green paper and stick it to the tab.

Make some more pages, moving subsequent tabs over ½" (1 cm) so they will all be visible when the book is bound. Use different colors for the small rectangles, stamping them with other veggies that grow in your garden.

To Bind the Booklet

Begin with an 8½" × 11" (22 cm × 28 cm) sheet of matte board and a 1½" x 11" (4 cm × 28 cm) strip of the same board. Stamp the board to coordinate with the booklet and to act as a background page. On the left side of the matte board, mark off a margin and use a three-hole punch to create holes so it can be inserted in your scrapbook. Starting at the top third of the matte board, glue the individual pages in place, moving each one down ½" to 1" (1 cm to 3 cm), depending on how many pages you have. When all the pages are in place, use an awl to punch through all the layers—the matte board, the pages, and the binding strip—and lace them with string or cord, tying a bow on the front. Don't pull tightly enough to cause friction on the holes. For viewing, you may want to untie the cord and loosen slightly while the pages are turned.

To Make the Page at Left

Use copy paper to mask a rectangle in the center of a sheet of bright green cardstock. This is where the tree will go. Use one or more bright green inkpads shaped like cat eyes or small cube pigment pads directly on the page, pressing down and swirling them in a random pattern over the cardstock. Ink a decorator leaf stamp with yellow or gold pigment ink, stamp over the top of the green, and let dry. Stamp the tree with sepia pigment ink and color the leaves and trunk with art pencils. Stamp letters on a sheet of buff parchment paper and draw a banner around them. Use art pencils to shade the folds of the banner, cut it out, and glue it over the tree.

QUICK TRICK

Use lettering to tie two facing pages together by running a continuous stream of words from one image to the next, crossing and weaving over the pages like a ribbon tying a package. See pages 44, 66, and 70.

Lettering

Lettering may take many forms on the pages of a scrapbook, and it serves several important purposes. Words and letters identify the subjects of photographs, putting names to the people who inhabit the pages. Words and letters can journal events or places and tell a story about the photographs. Letters can be embellished and colored, imparting beauty and meaning in the same way medieval illuminated manuscripts did before the printing press was invented. Lettering is used throughout the scrapbook and should be treated as any other element within its pages.

My Best Friends: Sticker Lettering

ARTIST: VICKI SCHREINER

On these two pages, the lettering continues from the left page across to the right, uniting them and unifying the designs.

STAMPING TRICK

Whenever possible, stamp words and letters on separate sheets of paper instead of stamping directly on the page. That way, you can choose the best stampings and cut them out to add to a completed scrapbook page without risking damage to your artwork.

MATERIALS

- **Stamps**
  Animal paw
  Cool cat
  Doggy Dalmatian
  Play ball
  Purrfect match
- **Ink and Inkpads**
  Black pigment inkpad
- **Paper**
  Two or three sheets each of white and black cardstock
  Two or three sheets of plaid paper
- **Miscellaneous**
  Assorted dye markers
  Fine-point black permanent marker
  Large red alphabet stickers
  Small black alphabet stickers

Getting Started

Stamp the black paw print randomly on white cardstock strips and allow to dry. Adhere the red letters over the paw prints. Use the black marker to outline the letters so they will stand out from the background.

Mounting the Words

Cut two strips of plaid background paper to form an even border behind each paw print strip and adhere the assemblage to the tops of two pages of printed or plain paper.

Finishing the Page

To finish the page, cut mats of plaid paper to form ½" (1 cm) borders all around the photos. Cut black mats the same size, and offset the plaid ones on top of them. Mount the photos in the centers of the plaid mats. Place the mounted photos on the page and add small black letters as desired. Stamp the cats and dogs on white cardstock and color with markers. Cut them out and stick them to the pages.

ARTIST: DAWN HOUSER

ABOVE: This example of lettering identifies the people in the photographs and also sets a whimsical mood for the entire page. Stamp the words on white cardstock and cut them out, then place them over the edges of photos and on the background. The arrangement of the words adds to the visual interest and variety of the page while keeping its light and playful tone.

Five Generations: Hand Lettered Pages

These two pages illustrate the beauty and intimacy that are possible with hand lettering. If your penmanship could use some help, it's worthwhile to invest some time and energy improving your hand. Many books on the subjects of calligraphy and hand lettering are available in bookstores.

ARTIST: VICKI SCHREINER

- **Stamps**

  Nostalgic key

  Nostalgic pocket watch

  Liquid amber leaf

- **Ink and Inkpads**

  Copper metallic inkpad

  Honeydew metallic inkpad

- **Paper**

  Natural parchment cardstock

- **Miscellaneous**

  Medium olive green and ochre fine-tip markers

  Squares and ovals templates

  Ivory vintage paper napkins

  Paper glue and glue pen

  Seagull paper edgers

QUICK TRICK

Should you decide to use your computer and printer for a faux handwriting font, try several different ones in various scripts and look for a style that is easy to read. When it comes to labeling your photographs, clarity is more important than ornamentation, and it's very easy to be carried away by the creativity that is found in fonts.

Getting Started

On a sheet of natural parchment, lightly draw the ovals for the names. Write the captions with the ochre fine tip marker, then go over the words again with the green. Make the green lettering slightly to the left of the ochre to create the illusion of shadows. Draw a green line around each oval and add dashed lines just inside it. Cut the ovals out and set aside for the final step.

Making the Pages

To make these vintage pages, stamp the background with the liquid amber leaf stamp and the honeydew pad on natural parchment cardstock. With the copper metallic ink, stamp about twenty keys on parchment cardstock, and stamp about fifteen pocket watches. Draw square and rectangle template shapes onto olive cardstock and also onto parchment. Make them about ½" (1 cm) larger all around than the photographs, then trim the parchment shapes slightly smaller than the olive. Mount the parchment shapes on the olive ones, then trim and mount the photographs on top of the parchment. Glue the small, framed photos to the background, cut out the keys and the pocket watches, and mount them at the sides and edges of the photos. To mat each of the large photographs, cut triangles from the corners of a paper lace napkin and butt them together to form a square. Tape lightly in the center to hold the square together, then mount the framed photograph on top. Glue the assemblage to the page. Add the captions to the appropriate photos. With seagull paper edgers, cut strips of olive cardstock and glue along the outside edges of the pages.

Love and Marriage: Mesh Lettered Pages

ARTIST: SUSAN JAWORSKI STRANC

These pages introduce a unique method for adding letters to your scrapbook. The artwork begins with a piece of wire grid with ⅜" mesh, but you may want to experiment with smaller and larger openings as well. Use wire cutters to snip the grid down to a workable size, about 3" × 4" (8 cm × 10 cm). Be sure to clip off all sharp, protruding wire points and flatten it completely. A 3" × 4" (8 cm × 10 cm) piece of fine, dense foam may be used with the grid to make the textured background.

NOTE: Various sizes and styles of mesh, available at stamping stores and from on-line merchants, may be used for this technique. If unavailable, you can use wire screening from the hardware store. Stamp stores also have heatable foam blocks which will accept the mesh pattern and which may be reheated to change the pattern as desired.

QUICK TRICK

For a rich, muted look in the photographs, experiment with your computer's photo program and try different screens as well as different colors. Color copiers can also print photos in a single color.

MATERIALS

- **Stamps**
  Small flower on a wooden dowel
  Tiny ivy garland
- **Ink and Inkpads**
  Gold metallic
  Black pigment
  Deep red pigment
- **Papers**
  Burgundy cardstock
  Gold metallic paper
  Burgundy textured art paper
- **Miscellaneous**
  3/8" mesh wire grid made for stamping
  Fine, dense heat-sensitive foam pad
  Wire cutters
  Heat tool

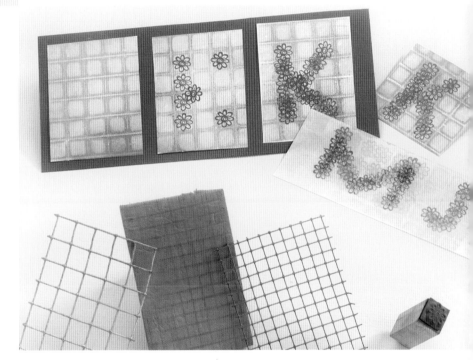

Getting Started

Method 1

Ink a block of heay-sensitive foam with gold metallic ink and lay it, inked side up, on the work surface. Place a piece of wire screen or mesh on top of the inked foam and lay a sheet of art paper or handmade paper on top of the screen. Gently press down on the paper with your fingertips, covering the entire surface and pressing it down into the ink beneath. Take care not to tear the paper by pressing too hard. For a variation, remove the paper and the mesh and stamp the foam onto a fresh piece of paper. Reink and repeat, to cover the page.

Method 2

Warm a block of heat-sensitive foam with a heat tool and press it onto the mesh to create a grid of raised squares on the foam. The impressions will remain until you reheat the foam. Ink the foam pad with gold metallic pigment ink and use it to stamp the page.

Stamping the Page

When the page has been covered with a grid of color, randomly stamp the tiny ivy garland pattern over the surface with red ink and then with black. Decide where your photos will go, then use the tiny flower to stamp the word "love" several times. You can form the letters by staying within the colored squares, or by stamping on the lines between the squares. To tie the pages together, let the word travel from the left page over onto the right side.

Finishing the Page

To finish the page, mount the photos on successively larger pieces of gold paper, burgundy textured paper, and gold paper again. Mount the photos at an angle on each page, noticing how they relate to one another when the pages are side by side.

To Make the Page at Left

Begin with a sheet of burnt orange cardstock or art paper. Remove the strips from a rainbow pigment inkpad one at a time and stamp them individually over the page, in a crisscross pattern. Stamp the letter on off-white parchment paper using brown ink. Use your fingertip to add more brown ink all around the edges of the letter, then cut it out. Glue it to the page at an angle. Fold a piece of silk ribbon or make a ribbon from orange paper. Heat a sealing wax disk and stamp with a sealer or small stamp that has been inked with gold metallic ink. Glue the ribbon along the edge of the letter and glue the wax seal on top. Stamp the individual letters with black ink on parchment paper and cut them out with deckle paper edgers. Arrange the letters into a word and glue them to a piece of brown cardstock. Cut the cardstock into a banner, darken the edges with brown ink, and glue in place.

NOTE: The letter on the page at left is a stamp. If you want to use an actual family letter or other document in the same way, scan it in color and print it on parchment paper. If you don't have the necessary equipment, take it to a copy center for color copies. Bring some parchment paper in case they don't carry it, and get several copies so you can experiment. Treat your copied letter the same as the stamped image.

Journaling

There are many ways to record thoughts, feelings, information, and memories in your scrapbook, and this chapter illustrates several of them. Some people keep elaborate daily journals where they record their lives in great detail. Others may write about special trips, events, or people. This book is more concerned with the addition of journaling to the pages of a scrapbook. The emphasis here is on the visual, whether it be photographs, stamping, artwork, or any other graphic aspect of keeping a scrapbook. There are many illustrations of journaling throughout the book. In this chapter, you will find three particular ways to document the events and people portrayed in the photographs. On page 74 there are two very diverse methods for adding words to a baby page and for preserving a grandfather's love letters. On page 76, the artist turns a trip to Paris into a double rebus page. And on page 78, words and images about a weekend in the mountains are creatively recorded in a booklet that fits into a scrapbook.

STAMPING TRICK

Most rainbow stamp pads can be taken apart so the individual colors can be stamped directly onto the paper. This is a good way to tie a page together and give it a unified look. Stamp the primary elements of the page with the rainbow pad, then use the individual colors on the background as well.

Vaughn Violet: Cut Out Words

These two scrapbook pages illustrate two methods of journaling. The sweet page for a baby girl contains words to illustrate the pride and love of her parents as they welcome her into their lives. The more somber and dignified page below embodies the love of a grandfather through his letters to his sweetheart when they were young. Both are versions of journaling, and each suits the mood and character of the photographs and other memorabilia.

Memories: A Preserved Letter

MATERIALS FOR VAUGHN VIOLET PAGE

- **Stamps**
  Large alphabet for name
  Small alphabet for words
  Corner with heart
  Heart
  Safety pin
  Lace edging
  Gingham checks
- **Ink and Inkpads**
  Clear and white embossing inkpads
  Silver, white, clear, and sparkle embossing powders
  Pink, deep lavender, and white pigment inks
- **Papers**
  Three sheets of pink cardstock
  Three sheets of white cardstock
- **Miscellaneous**
  Very sharp pointed scissors
  Fine silver cord
  Awl or small round hole punch

MATERIALS FOR MEMORIES PAGE

- **Stamps**
  Fancy Bollio flourish
- **Ink and Inkpads**
  Eggshell white pigment ink
- **Papers**
  Black cardstock
  Vintage photos on printed paper
- **Miscellaneous**
  Sepia silk ribbon
  Gold key and heart charms
  Gold cord

Getting Started

Stamp a sheet of white cardstock with the gingham checks and pink pigment ink, repeating as needed to cover the page. It may be easier to line up the checks if you stamp the entire page, instead of leaving blank space in the center for the photos. Stamp a sheet of pink cardstock with the lace stamp and white pigment ink, then emboss with white embossing powder before it dries. Stamp the lace in strips down the sheet, leaving at least ½" (1 cm) between them. Cut one edge of each strip straight, then use the precision pointed scissors to cut out the points along the opposite edges. Miter the corners and glue the strips around the gingham page to create a lacy frame. Use the awl or the punch to make holes at the inner edge of the lace frame, going through the lace and the gingham sheet.

Mounting the Photos

Mount the photographs on pink cardstock, trim to a narrow margin around each one, and glue in place on the page. Stamp eight corners with clear embossing ink on pink cardstock and emboss with silver powder. Cut them out and mount over each photo corner.

Adding the Words

Stamp the small words on a sheet of white cardstock using black ink. Stamp four hearts and two safety pins on pink or white paper, then emboss one side of some of them with clear embossing ink and sparkle embossing powder. Stamp the baby's name with large letters and deep lavender ink on white cardstock. Cut out the words, the hearts, and the safety pins.

Finishing the Page

Thread the silver cord through the punched holes, leaving long tails. Tie a loose bow and attach the cutouts to the ends of the cord. Glue the baby's name beneath the photos and some of the small words randomly around the page. Stamp and emboss a few safety pins along the right and top edges of the page.

Making the Memories Page

Stamp the Bollio flourish all around the border of the black cardstock using eggshell pigment ink. Trim the vintage photo paper to about 6½" × 9" (17 cm × 23 cm) and round off the corners. Mount the paper in the center of the cardstock. Lay the ribbon across the page, glue about 2"–3" (5 cm–8 cm) of the center of the ribbon to the center of the page, and let dry. Place the folded love letters and the photo on top of the ribbon and tie into a bow. Tie the charms on the ribbon with the gold cord.

STAMPING TRICK

To preserve your precious old letters, have them photocopied onto parchment paper and use those in your scrapbook, keeping the originals in a safe place. To age the copied letters, brush sepia ink around the edges. If you have an old photo, but no love letters, stamp some parchment paper with a script stamp and create a love story.

Paris Dream Trip: Rebus Story Pages

A trip to Paris presented this artist with the chance of a lifetime. She turned the trip into a rebus story on two stamped pages of words and images. A rebus story is created when you substitute symbols, pictures, and graphics for some of the words in a narrative.

To document your own trip, collect postcards, regional and other representative stamps, tickets, photographs, and other memorabilia that symbolize the place, its mood and theme.

MATERIALS

- **Stamps**

  Travel Bollio

  Baggage

  Compass

  French postcards

  DeGaulle

  Corner script, C. Leroux

  France block

  Flight instrument

  St. Louis skyline

  "Dream"

  "Paris"

  "Visit to Paris"

  Stamp cancel

  Eiffel tower

  Small Eiffel tower

  Maps and visas

- **Ink and Inkpads**

  Lavender, neptune, and stone gray pigment

  Permanent black

- **Papers**

  Two or three sheets each of black, white, and pearl gray cardstock

  One sheet of lightweight clear vellum

- **Miscellaneous**

  Stipple brushes

  Art pencils

  Laminating machine with adhesive cartridge (optional)

  Purple gel pen or fine tip marker

Getting Started

Stamp the gray cardstock with the smaller stamps, overlapping and turning them at various angles. Use stone gray ink to create a shadow effect over both backgrounds. With the stipple brushes, shade and stipple neptune and lavender over the stamped backgrounds. Cut the photos into interesting shapes and attach them to the white cardstock and mount on the page. Stamp the larger images on white cardstock, color with the art pencils, cut out, and attach to the page. Arrange the photos, the stampings, and other elements so that words may be interspersed between and around them, and add words with a purple gel pen.

To Make the Luggage

Stamp the bag on a square of vellum using black ink and let dry. Color with art pencils from the back side. Trim with paper edgers and adhere to the page.

To Make the Corner Pocket

In the lower left corner, stamp the corner script image then cut along the inner edge with a craft knife to form a place for tickets, photos, and other loose memorabilia to be tucked in. Trim ¼" (5 mm) from each edge of the completed pages and mount on black cardstock. This will frame the pages and create a backing for the corner pocket so items won't fall through.

STAMPING TRICK

Before you begin stamping a rebus page, collect photos, memorabilia, maps, postcards, and other elements to express the theme. Lay them out on a sheet of paper and move them around to jump-start a story. Next, look for stamps that will add to the story line and liven up the page. Choose word stamps, letter stamps, and images in a variety of sizes and styles. Make a test page by stamping the words and images around the photos before gluing them down.

Mountain Cabin Retreat: A Journaling Booklet

ARTIST: SUSAN JAWORSKI STRANC

This two-page booklet is a prime example of journaling. The artist and friends spent several days at a mountain cabin, not only enjoying their time and the atmosphere, but also writing about the experience.

Constructing this booklet is much simpler than it first appears. A double sheet (17" × 11" [43 cm × 28 cm]) of art paper is the starting point.

MATERIALS

- **Stamps**

  All the stamps are handmade from air-dry modeling clay and fine sponges, or are hand carved as described in the Basics section (page 12)

- **Ink and Inkpads**

  Dye ink in a full range of colors

- **Papers**

  Light charcoal gray art paper, 11" × 17" (28 cm × 43 cm)

  White charcoal or watercolor paper, 11" × 17" (28 cm × 43 cm)

  Beige or tan paper ribbon

- **Miscellaneous**

  Air-dry modeling clay

  Fine sponges, about ½" (1 cm) thick

  Cookie cutters

  Rolling pin, glass quart jar, or other roller for clay

  Black permanent writing pen with very fine point

To make the people stamps, roll out some air-dry modeling compound and cut it with cookie cutters. Let dry overnight and use as stamps. For trees, cut some fine sponge into triangles and gouge out the lines with stamp carving tools.

Getting Started

Begin by creating simple leaf stamps from stamp carving supplies as described in the Basics section, page 12. Make some air-dry clay stamps, also described in the Basics section. Stamp the large sheet or gray paper randomly with carved leaf stamps, adding a few small rubber-stamped leaves in rust or burgundy.

Making the Pages

For each journaling page, cut or tear a strip of white paper about 4" (10 cm) wide by 17" (43 cm) long. At the top of each strip, create a scene to go with your story using handmade clay or sponge stamps. Below that, attach a photograph or two, keeping in mind where the strip will fold back into the page. Stamp a few impressions on the back of the strip. Over the stamping, write a journal entry about the scene and the photos, including what the day was like and what you did. To make the pages even more interesting, don't write in a straight line. Curve the lines, make squares with them, write in circles, and create other interesting patterns with the words.

ABOVE: Photos and journaling are applied to smaller sheets as foldout pages and are attached to the large basic page.

Putting the Booklet Together

Score the back of each strip about 1" (3 cm) from the top and glue to the large page only along the top 1" (3 cm) of the strip so it will fold. When all the strip pages are mounted, fold the large page in half like a book. Punch holes for inserting the closed page into a three-ring binder, cut slits near each hole, and run a flattened strip of tan paper ribbon through each one to fan out on the inside surface of the pages.

ARTIST: BETTY AUTH

To Create the Page at Left

Begin with a sheet of tan cardstock. Stamp the fancy frame near the bottom center of the page and emboss it with gold. Randomly stamp the star with bronze dye ink around the page and in the center of the frame with red dye or embossing ink then emboss with bronze. Stamp the letters with red pigment ink on gold vellum, then cut them out and apply to another sheet of vellum in a wavy line. Cut the vellum into a flag and daub the edges with gold. Daub a wooden skewer with gold and let dry. Tear a piece of white handmade paper and glue it to the upper portion of the page, glue the flag over it, and add the skewer. Weight the skewer and allow to dry before moving the page.

QUICK TRICK

Add a more personal touch to your scrapbook pages by writing or drawing with a two-way glue pen or a bottle of fabric paint equipped with a fine tip applicator. While the glue or paint is still wet, sprinkle with embossing powder and set with a heat tool. You can write names and dates, or draw small hearts, flowers, and other simple shapes.

Dividers

Creating divider pages can organize a scrapbook into different sections. Pages 82 and 83 show two examples of dividers that identify the theme of the pages to follow. The Mothers and Daughters theme could refer to more photographs of this particular duo, and could record their lives together over the years. It could also indicate that the section contains a collection of different moms and kids, or grandmothers with their mothers.

Fun with Mom: A Mother/Daughter Page

ARTIST: DAWN HOUSER

Although this page is shown as a left-hand scrapbook page, it could also be mounted on the right and become a dividing page for the section to follow.

Evan and Haley:
Illuminated Letters

MATERIALS FOR MOTHER/DAUGHTER PAGE

- **Stamps**
  - Background block with metro theme
  - Butterfly with zebra wings
  - Alphabet
  - Shoes
  - Party dress
- **Ink and Inkpads**
  - Black, charcoal, pink, magenta, blue-violet, and red pigment inks
  - Charcoal, black, and sparkle embossing powders
- **Papers**
  - Two sheets of turquoise cardstock
  - Scraps of white, pink, and lavender cardstock
- **Miscellaneous**
  - Stippling brush

To Make the Mother/Daughter Page

Stamp an entire sheet of turquoise cardstock with the metro stamp and charcoal pigment ink. Stamp the individual letters for the words with black or clear pigment ink on various pastel colors of cardstock and emboss with charcoal powder. Do only two or three letters at a time so they won't dry out before the embossing powder is added. Cut out the letters and set aside. Stamp the four butterflies, the dresses, and the shoes on white or pastel cardstock, then emboss as you choose. Cut them out. Cut pieces of black or pastel cardstock slightly larger than the photos and mount the photos on the pieces of cardstock to create slender frames. Mount the photos on the page, then add the other elements.

MATERIALS FOR BABY PAGE

- **Stamps**
  - Bollio with flower theme
  - Illuminated alphabet blocks
- **Ink and Inkpads**
  - Pine green dye ink
  - Scarlet and forest green pigment ink
  - Pastel embossing powder
- **Papers**
  - Three sheets of ivory cardstock
- **Miscellaneous**
  - Transparent ruler for placing letters
  - Oval cutter (optional)
  - Pastel markers

ARTIST: pj DUTTON

To Make the Baby Page

Using pine green ink, stamp the flower Bollio along the top and bottom of a sheet of ivory cardstock. Color the leaves and flowers with markers. Trim the photograph into an oval and mount it in the center of the page.

Stamping the Names

On a separate sheet of ivory cardstock, stamp the individual illuminated letters for the names, using scarlet for the girl and forest green for the boy. Doing one or two at a time, emboss the letters with pastel embossing powder before the ink has dried. Color the letters and embellish with markers—this will make them pink and blue. Cut out each letter and use the transparent ruler to help in gluing them evenly around the photo. Note that the letters in the boy's name are just touching each other, while the girl's are overlapping because there are more letters in hers.

Time Flies By: A Heritage Divider Page

Getting Started

Beginning with the lightest ink color, randomly stamp some dragonflies on a sheet of green cardstock, turning them in various directions. Continue stamping dragonflies with successively darker and brighter colors until the page is covered. Stamp and emboss three or four more dragonflies on white cardstock. Color the embossed images with watercolor pencils and daub some of the background colors on the bodies. Cut out the embossed dragonflies.

QUICK TRICK

To make an element stand out from the background, use foam-centered sticky dots to mount it, raising it above the surface of the page.

MATERIALS

- **Stamps**

  Dragonfly

- **Ink and Inkpads**

  Pink, fuchsia, lavender, and purple pigment cubes

  Clear embossing ink and sparkle powder

- **Papers**

  One sheet of medium green cardstock

  One sheet of white cardstock

- **Miscellaneous**

  Double-sided sticky dots

  Watercolor pencils

  Small paintbrush

  Sponge or sponge dauber

  Computer with script font or black fine-tip marker for hand lettering

Finishing the Page

Print the words on white cardstock, by hand or with a computer, and cut them out as a banner. Trim the photos and mount them in the center of the page, overlapping and fanning them out. Mount the banner above them. Use sticky dots to attach the dragonflies so they will stand out.

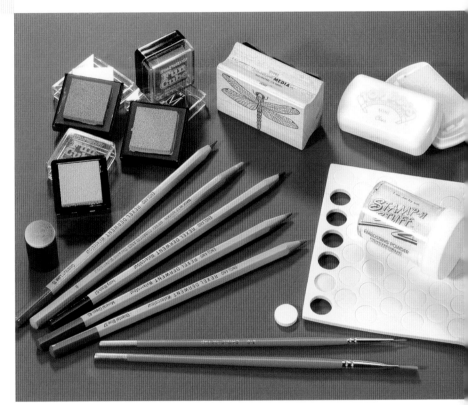

Watercolor pencils are effective tools for scrapbook pages because you can control the amount of water on the brush and avoid wrinkling the page.

My All Stars: Booklet as Divider

The cover of this little booklet says, "My All Stars."

There are no rules governing the format for divider pages, so why not start a section on school, or sports, or the kids in general, with a fold-out booklet. The pages that follow it might contain more photographs and memorabilia pertaining to any of the above subjects, with this page acting as the introduction to the section.

ARTIST: pj DUTTON

- **Stamps**
  Filmstrip
  Jeans pocket
  Alphabet
- **Ink and Inkpads**
  Coal and indigo inkpads
- **Papers**
  Three sheets each of red and white cardstock
  Two sheets of baseball-printed paper
  Three 5½" (14 cm) square red greeting cards (or cut from three
  additional sheets of red cardstock)
  Tracing paper
- **Miscellaneous**
  Bone folder for creasing
  Circle and star cutters or punches (optional)

NOTE: If circle and star cutters or punches are not available, draw the shapes on the card-stock and photos and cut them out.

Getting Started

To make the background page, trim the baseball paper to 8" × 10½" (20 cm × 27 cm) and layer it onto a sheet of red cardstock. Cut three 2⅛" (5 cm) red cardstock circles and three 2" (5 cm) round photos, then mount the photos on the red circles. Attach across the top of the baseball page.

Making the Booklet

To create the booklet, use transparent (not translucent) tape to attach the red cards together to form an accordion strip. On some of the folded pages, mount smaller versions of the round photos that are at the top of the background page. On other pages, use the following techniques to create frames for photographs.

Method #1

Stamp the filmstrip on white cardstock using coal ink. Stamp a second time on tracing paper, then cut out one of the tracing paper photo spaces for a pattern. Lay the pattern over your photo, mark around it, then cut out the photo and mount it on the white cardstock filmstrip.

Method #2

To turn the jeans pocket into a frame, stamp it with indigo ink on white cardstock. Use a craft knife to cut out a window and mount the photo behind the opening. This could be done with the filmstrip, but the frames are very fragile and easy to tear.

STAMPING TRICK

When stamping a large block image like the jeans pocket, try it first on scrap paper, pressing down across its surface with your fingertips. Take care not to move the stamp; let it rest for a few seconds on the page then lift straight up.

Here are two methods for adding photographs to a stamped page. The larger photo on the right will go into the opening in the jeans pocket.

Stamping the Words

If your alphabet stamps do not have frames around them, stamp each letter separately on white cardstock, cut them out separately, then use a stipple brush or a sponge to darken the edges with indigo ink. Attach the words to the front page of the booklet and add names to each of the photos inside. Mount the folded booklet on the background page and crease well so it will lie flat.

COVERS

To Make the Page at Left

Stamp a piece of neutral cardstock with a large flower stamp and two or three colors of pigment ink, leaving lots of blank space. Stamp three more flowers on a sheet of heavy translucent vellum and emboss with clear powder. Trim 1" (3 cm) off each edge of the vellum with straight scissors. Use decorative paper edgers to embellish the edges of the vellum. Stamp the word on a piece of white or cream cardstock using black dye ink. Cut the word out of the cardstock with paper edgers and glue it on the vellum sheet with a glue stick. Glue the vellum over the background sheet along the top edge only, and cut a strip of white or cream cardstock to cover the glued area at the top of the overleaf.

NOTE: This page uses pigment ink on vellum, although dye ink usually works best. Pigment ink must dry for a long time, and sometimes the images are not solidly colored because the ink can bead. Heavier vellum may be embossed or the heat tool used to shorten drying time; heat can buckle the lighter weight vellums.

ARTIST: BETTY AUTH

Covers

When all your beautiful scrapbook pages are finished, you will want a gorgeous cover for the album that holds them. In this chapter you'll find many different themes and techniques so you can choose the methods and the looks that best represent your photographs and scrapbook pages. Sometimes you may want to make the pages first then construct an appropriate cover, while at other times you might prefer creating the entire album and cover at once. Either way is fine, and it comes down to personal preference.

QUICK TRICK

When working with vellum, use a glue stick instead of wet adhesive because vellum wrinkles easily when wet. If it does wrinkle, cover the glued area with an embellishment.

Paris Journal: Mica Chip Cover

ARTIST: pj DUTTON

Here is a way to embellish the cover of a purchased blank journal so it is as beautiful and as important as the words within.

MATERIALS

- **Stamps**

  "Paris 1920"

  "Travel Journal"

  Postage and travel stamps

- **Ink and Inkpads**

  Black pigment ink

- **Papers**

  Cream or neutral handmade paper, 11" × 17" (28 cm × 43 cm)

  One sheet of cream cardstock

- **Miscellaneous**

  Large mica chips (embossing tiles)

  Fine gold or copper wire

  Wire cutters

  Round-nose pliers

  Drill with $^1/_{16}$-inch (1.5 mm) drill bit

  Paper adhesive

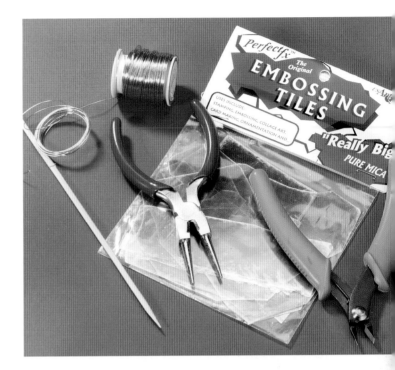

Getting Started

Stamp the large sheet of handmade paper randomly with black ink, using all of the stamps except the words "Travel Journal." Cover a purchased blank journal with the stamped paper. Stamp the travel images onto cardstock and cut them out, forming 3"–4" (8 cm–10 cm) rectangles and squares. Stamp the words "Travel Journal" on cardstock and cut them out. Glue the words and the images onto the paper cover as shown in the photograph.

When curling wire, use round nose pliers, not needle nose, and either curl the wire around the pliers themselves or around a knitting needle or wooden skewer.

Making the Mica Embellishments

Cut the large mica chips into pieces that will cover the cardstock stampings. Lay the mica pieces on a flat surface and stamp them, leaving the centers of the mica chips clear so you can see the images underneath. Open the cover of the journal and lay it on a piece of scrap wood with the mica pieces in places. Drill a few holes through the mica and the journal cover.

Finishing the Cover

To wire the mica chips on the cover, coil about ½" (1 cm) of wire in one end of an 8" (20 cm) length of wire. Push the straight end through the cover, the handmade paper, and the mica from the inside. Trim to 1" (3 cm) and coil that end on the front of the journal. Bend and mash the coils so they lay flat against the surface.

STAMPING TRICK

When planning a vacation or other trip, buy a couple of blank journals to take along and record your thoughts and memories as you go. Leave plenty of space on the pages and tuck your favorite memorabilia into the journal with your words. When you come home, finish up the journal with rubber stamps, handmade stamps, and other techniques found throughout this book. Make a rebus page. Stamp a cover. Stamp some frames, borders, and background papers to add, then tie it together with a ribbon.

By the Shore: Beaded Album Cover

A layered and embellished cover such as this one promises marvelous surprises within and it honors the time that these friends spent together on their seaside vacation.

ARTIST: SANDRA McCALL

MATERIALS

- **Stamps**

  Leaves

  Hearts

  Textures and other elements

- **Ink and Inkpads**

  Reinkers in purple, green, blue, fuchsia and

  turquoise

- **Papers**

  Matte board

  Three sheets of monoprint, faux batik or

  handmade paper (Refer to the Basics section, page

  11, for instructions on making these papers)

- **Miscellaneous**

  Metallic bead strings and flower strings

  Gold metallic cord

  Seaside trinkets and leaf sprays

  Frosted sea glass

  Permanent bonding adhesive or thick white craft glue

  Glue stick

  Craft scissors or clippers

QUICK TRICK

To create pages like these, you will need scraps and partial pages of decorative paper. Leaf through this book and try some of the techniques, then save the papers you create in a folder, a box, or a book for later use.

Step 1

Cut an 8 ½" × 11" (22 cm × 28 cm) piece of matte board and cover it with a sheet of decorative paper to provide a sturdy background. Either wrap the paper around the edges of the board to the back and cover the back with another piece of paper, or cut the paper the same size as the matte board, mount it, and color the edges of the board with markers.

Step 2

Cut an additional piece of matte board about 2" (5 cm) larger all around than the photographs and cover it with a coordinating piece of decorative paper.

Step 3

Cut a frame for the photos from matte board and cover it with handmade or decorative paper. Make the frame windows about ½" (1 cm) larger all around than the photographs.

Step 4

Cut small matte boards the same size as the photos. Mount the photos on the small matte boards and color the edges with markers to coordinate with the background.

Step 5

Assemble the pieces in the same order in which they were made, referring to the project photo at left for placement.

Step 6

Embellish the layers with bead strings, gold cord, and flower strings. Use the permanent bonding adhesive to glue the beads and trinkets in the center of the cover. Hint: Be sure to cut the bead and flower strings accurately so they will fit where they meet at the corners and hold them in the glue until it sets.

KARI LEE FOR THE LEATHER FACTORY;
HOUSTON, TEXAS

This large 14" (36 cm) square wooden album has been covered with leather and stamped with the letter "L" encased in a simple stamped frame. Suede strips are stamped with a checkerboard pattern and colored with markers then wrapped around the album's edges.

SUNN SHIPTON FOR DEEP IMPRESSIONS;
VICTORIA, AUSTRALIA

This album cover illustrates an easy and effective way to use a flat scrapbook page as a cover for an album or journal. There are five layers of paper in its construction. The lavender and white layers are embellished first, with stamps from Deep Impressions. The pieces are cut to the proper size and shape, then laid on the lavender background and the entire piece is mounted on the album. The artist used fiberglass paper for the small white square, but any textured white handmade paper would work.

SUSAN JAWORSKI STRANC, APPLE CIDER PRESS;
NEWBURY, MASSACHUSETTS

Handmade and hand-painted papers set these beautiful albums apart as stylish and
fitting containers for treasures and memories. The spines are embellished with beads
and cord, ending in tassels, and the albums fit precisely into coordinating handmade
slip cases for protection. Sets are available from the artist.

BETTY AUTH, AUTH-ANTIC DESIGNS; HOUSTON, TEXAS

Two ready-made wooden albums are decorated with stamps, then woodburned and colored with oil pencils and stamping inks. The smaller one has been stamped through a mesh to create the grid, and some embossing powder appears on two of the brass charm hummingbirds. The twigs are from the artist's backyard.

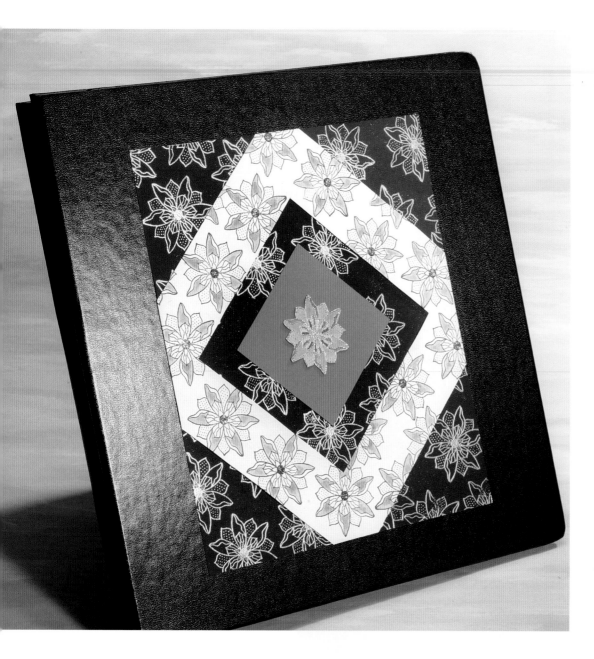

SUNN SHIPTON FOR DEEP IMPRESSIONS;
VICTORIA, AUSTRALIA

*Almost any scrapbook could be enhanced by the addition of this gorgeous album
cover. A single Deep Impressions stamp is used on a sheet of black cardstock, stamped
and embossed in silver. The same image is then repeated in the center in contrasting
colors. The white diamond shape is stamped in blue to coordinate with the center
blue square. The whole assembly is turned on point for a striking design.*

SUNN SHIPTON FOR DEEP IMPRESSIONS;
VICTORIA, AUSTRALIA

These two album covers make effective use of every bit of space. Prominent black squares down the center of the beige cover are offset by deeply embossed red and white corners. On the family album, round stamps from Deep Impressions form a border and are colored with markers. The addition of a bow and tassels on the upper corner of the album accentuates the colors.

VICKI SCHREINER, VICKI'S ORIGINALS;
SPRINGFIELD, MISSOURI

*In this example, the pieces are shown before assembly to illustrate how easy it is to
create an album from a wooden frame. Cut a spine from a scrap of wood the same
thickness as the frame, then cut a thinner wooden back the same size as the combined
frame and spine. Finish the raw wood to match the frame and put it together with
tiny hinges and screws. The frame is stamped, wood-burned, colored with oil pencils,
and stained pale green. All wooden pieces should be varnished to prevent warping.*

SUNN SHIPTON FOR DEEP IMPRESSIONS;
VICTORIA, AUSTRALIA

Black foam core board was used to make this cover, which was mounted on the front of the album after holes were punched for the chiffon ribbon. The foam core used here is black all the way through, so there are no white edges to worry about. The graceful Asian motifs from Deep Impressions are enhanced with fine silver embossing and the centerpiece is embossed with rainbow powder. Muted colors are added with markers to soften the starkness of the black and silver border.

SUNN SHIPTON FOR DEEP IMPRESSIONS;
VICTORIA, AUSTRALIA

This little mini-book is a gem, and would enhance the sentiments of anyone who used it for recording their thoughts. Outside, the Deep Impressions stamps are heavily embossed with white so they stand out against the red background. The images in the center are highlighted with markers against a blue rectangle, and the blue is repeated inside the cover. The accordion pages are outlined with another image in black dye ink, adding further meaning and depth to them.

KARI LEE FOR THE LEATHER FACTORY;
HOUSTON, TEXAS

These three little frame albums are all constructed in a similar fashion. They are purchased leather frames equipped with stands so they can lay flat or stand up on a table. The leather is dyed and then stamped with images to complement each photograph. The stampings are colored with markers and the albums are joined with leather lacing tied in knots along the spines. Blank frames are available from The Leather Factory.

Resources

NORTH AMERICA

Angelwings Enterprises
3065 North Sunnyside #101
Fresno, CA 93727
PHONE: 800.400.3717
www.radiantpearls.com
Radiant Pearls translucent, pearlized
paint

Artistic Wire
1210 Harrison Avenue
LaGrange Park, IL 60526
PHONE: 630.530.7567
FAX: 630.530.7536
www.artisticwire.com
colored copper wire, tools, accessories

Binney & Smith
1100 Church lane
Easton, PA 18044
www.binney-smith.com
distributors of Crayola and Liquitex products, Model Magic modeling compound

Clearsnap, Inc.
Box 98
Anacortes, WA 98221
PHONE: 800.448.4862
FAX: 360.293.6699
www.clearsnap.com
pens, inks, stamps, accessories .

Creative Paperclay
79 Daily Drive, Suite 101
Camarillo, CA 93010
PHONE: 805.484.6648
FAX: 805.484.8788
www.creativepaperclay.com
air-dry clay

DMD Industries
2300 South Old Missouri Rd.
Springdale, AR 72764
PHONE: 800.805.9890
FAX: 501.750.8937
www.dmdind.com
paper, journals, albums

Fiskars, Inc.
7811 W. Stewart Ave.
Wausau, WI 54401
www.fiskars.com
scissors, paper edgers, cutters, accessories

Hero Arts
1343 Powell Street
Emeryville, CA 94608
PHONE: 510.652.6055
www.heroarts.com
rubber stamps, sets, accessories

Inkadinkado
61 Holton Street
Woburn, MA 01801
www.inkadinkado.com
Daydreams Collection by Dawn Houser,
other rubber stamps

Judi-Kins
17803 S. Harvard Blvd.
Gardena, CA 90248
www.judi-kins.com
cube stamps, Bollios, Diamond Glaze,
crackle stamp, other rubber stamps

Magenta Rubber Stamps
351 Rue Blain
Mont Saint Hilaire
Quebec J3H 3B4
Canada
PHONE: 450.922.5253
FAX: 450.922.0053
www.magentarubberstamps.com
art stamps, papers, cards, scrapbooks, more

Marvy-Uchida
3535 Del Amo Blvd.
Torrance, CA 90503
PHONE: 800.541.5877
FAX: 800.229.7017
www.uchida.com
fabric, paper, opaque markers

Paper Adventures
P.O. Box 04393
Milwaukee, WI 53204
PHONE: 800.727.0699
FAX: 800.727.0268
www.paperadventures.com
art and scrapbooking papers

Papers by Catherine
11328 South Post Oak Road #108
Houston, TX 77035
PHONE: 713.723.3334
FAX: 713.723.4749
www.papersbycatherine.com
vellum, handmade and art papers

Personal Stamp Exchange
360 Sutton Place
Santa Rosa, CA 95407
PHONE: 707.588.8058
FAX: 707.588.7476
www.psxstamps.com
rubber stamps, stickers, accessories

Ranger Industries
15 Park Rd.
Tinton Falls, NJ 07724
PHONE: 732.389.3535
FAX: 732.389.1102
www.rangerink.com
ink, inkpads, stamping accessories

Rubber Stampede
Delta Technical Coatings
2550 Pellissier Place
Whittier, CA 90601
www.rubberstampede.com
stamps, inkpads, Curve Décor stamping
systems, accessories

Stampers Anonymous
20613 Center Ridge Road
Rocky River, OH 44116
PHONE: 440.333.7941
FAX: 440.333.7992
www.stampersanonymous.com
stamps, papers, inks, accessories

Stampington & Company
22992 Mill Creek Drive
Ste. B
Laguna Hills, CA 92647
PHONE: 949.380.7318
FAX: 949.380.9355
www.stampington.com
art stamps, books, magazines
(Somerset Studio), accessories

Sunday International
5672 Buckingham Drive
Huntington Beach, CA 92649
PHONE: 800.401.8644 (orders only)
www.sundayint.com
rubber stamps, accessories

Tidy Crafts
1330 Enterprise
Idaho Falls, ID 83402
PHONE: 208.523.2565
www.tidycrafts.com
Tidy Trays, organizing accessories

Toner Plastics, Inc.
699 Silver Street
Agawam, MA 01001
PHONE: 413.789.1300
FAX: 413.789.1144
www.tonerplastics.com
colored plastic art wire

Tsukineko
15411 N.E. Ninety-fifth Street
Redmond, WA 98052
PHONE: 800.769.6633
www.tsukineko.com
inks, inkpads, markers, pens

US ArtQuest, Inc.
7800 Ann Arbor Road
Grass Lake, MI 49240
PHONE: 517.522.6225
FAX: 517.522.6228
www.usartquest.com
Perfect Paper adhesive

Walnut Hollow
1409 State Road 23
Dodgeville, WI 53533
PHONE: 800.950.5101
www.walnuthollow.com
woodburners, unfinished wooden
albums, oil color pencils

Xyron Inc.
15820 North 84th Street
Scottsdale, AZ 85260
PHONE: 800.793.3523
www.xyron.com
laminating and sticker machines and
cartridges

AUSTRALIA
Stamp and Supply Stores

NEW SOUTH WALES
Fantasy Craft Stamps
224 Brunker Road
Adamstown NSW 2289
PHONE: 02.4957.2255

Stampmania
Shop 6 Alexandria Street
Berry NSW 2535
PHONE: 02.4464.2677
EMAIL: Stampmania@Shoal.net.au

The Rubber Stamp Shop
37 Beach Street
Wollongong NSW 2500
PHONE: 02.4229.6594
EMAIL: Imprint@Hotkey.net.au

The Stampers Garage
50 Anchorage Street
Erskine Park NSW 2759
PHONE: 02.8803.0896
EMAIL:
Thestampersgarage@Goconnect.net

Stamp in Style
376 Forest Road
Bexley NSW 2207
PHONE: 02.9597.2676
EMAIL: Stampinstyle@Optusnet.com.au

My Stamping Ground
Top Of The Town
Shop 3/133 Princes Hwy
Ulladulla NSW 2539
PHONE: 02.4454.3260

QUEENSLAND
Lucy's Stamps
30 Macaranga Street
Marsden QLD 4132
PHONE: 07.3805.1115

Elizabeth Lee Country Stamps
42 Phillipson Road
Charters Towers QLD 4820
PHONE: 07.4787.3712

A Stamper's Friend
16 Foothill Street
Elanora QLD 4221
PHONE: 07.5534.6506
EMAIL: sharmies@one.net.au

Impressive Stamps Australia
13 Agnew Street
Norman Park QLD 4170
PHONE: 07.3399.3737
EMAIL: Berni@Tpg.com.au

Stampers Heaven
Shop 5
257 Stafford Road
Stafford QLD 4053
PHONE: 07.3857.7799

Black Cat Creations
P O Box 489
Everton Park QLD 4053
PHONE: 07.3354.4411

Bumble Bee Crafts
7 Toolara Street
The Gap QLD 4061
PHONE: 07.3511.0068
EMAIL: Buzz@Gil.com.au

Creative Art Stamps
399 Honour Avenue
Graceville QLD 4075
PHONE: 07.3278.2814

Handstamped Art—Australia
P O Box 439n
North Cairns QLD 4870
PHONE: 07.4057.5812
EMAIL: Handstamped@lig.com.au

Platypus Creek Stamping & Craft
Shop 3 Stanto Place (Cnr Stanton
Rd & Captain Cook Hwy)
Smithfield QLD
PHONE: 07.4038.1013
EMAIL: Platycreek@Bigpond.com

SOUTH AUSTRALIA
Annaleey Crafts
P O Box 66
Yeelanna SA 5632
PHONE: 08.8676.5026
EMAIL:
Stamps@Annaleeycrafts.com.au

Aussie Stamps & Crafts
4 Brougham Place
Golden Grove SA 5125
PHONE: 08.8289.8871
EMAIL: Mwo@Iweb.net.au

Dream Mode
Po Box 338
Tailem Bend SA 5260
PHONE: 08.8572.3553

TASMANIA
Gail's Stamps & Crafts
22 Binney Street
Ravenswood TAS 7250
PHONE: 03.6339.2002
EMAIL: Fsargent@Our.net.au

The Stamping Bug Gift Shop
Shop 8/39 Wragg Street
Somerset TAS 7322
PHONE: 03.6435.0603
EMAIL:
Stampingbug@Bigpond.com.au

VICTORIA
Stampalot
Cnr Main & Barkly Streets
Mornington VIC 3931
PHONE: 03.5975.8550

Cambrae Stamps
Shop 36, The Gateway Village
230 Cranbourne Road
Langwarrin VIC 3910
PHONE: 03.8790.8217
EMAIL: Cambraestamps@Netstra.com.au

Deep Impressions
1/38 Nepean Avenue
Moorabbin VIC 3189
PHONE: 03.9773.5889
EMAIL: Impressions@hotvoice.com

Little Bits
389 Chandler Road
Keysborough VIC 3173
PHONE: 03.9798.4122

The Creative Stamp Collection Pty Ltd
6-10 Kepple Street
Shepparton VIC 3630
PHONE: 03.5831.3233

Rivendell Cottage
109 Ryrie Street
Geelong VIC 3220
PHONE: 03.5224.1911

WESTERN AUSTRALIA
The Rubber Stamp Company
Shop 4, 1919 Albany Highway
Maddington WA 6109
PHONE: 08.9493.2730

South West Rubber Stamps
Shop 9 Koombana Court
141 Victoria Street
Bunbury WA 6230
PHONE: 08.9791.5050

Stamp-It Rubber Stamps
276 Albany Highway
Victoria Park WA 6100
PHONE: 08.9470.5422
EMAIL: Stamps@Stampit.com.au

ART STAMP COMPANIES
Collections Rubber Stamps
6 Alisa Court
Alexander Heights WA 6064
PHONE: 08.9247.3665

Lucy's Stamps
30 Macaranga Street
Marsden QLD 4132
PHONE: 07.3805.1115
FAX: 07.3805.9095

Contributing Artists

pj Dutton – pp. 26, 28, 34, 44, 74, 76, 83, 86, 90
pj dutton prefers that her name not be capitalized. She lives in Festus, Missouri, and teaches classes in stamping and related paper arts throughout the country. pj's work has appeared in many major stamping magazines, and in books such as *Stamp Art* by Sharilyn Miller, Rockport Publishers. pj has authored three books about stamping on and creating with vellum, and she does sample cards for Judi-Kins and Stampers Anonymous rubber stamp companies.
pj may be contacted at:
636-931-2613
email: PJSTAMPS@aol.com

Dawn Houser – pp. 22, 38, 52, 67, 74, 82
Both a full-time graphic designer and a mother of three, Dawn Houser creates images that are sophisticated and charming. Her designs evoke a mix of today and yesteryear. Dawn licenses her images to various companies in different media and does freelance design work for individuals and companies. Dawn's Daydreams line of stamps may be seen at Inkadinkado and her die cut designs at Accu-Cut Systems.
Dawn may be contacted at:
210-930-0373
Web: www.dawnhouser.com
email: howzr@aol.com

Sandra McCall – pp. 20, 30, 36, 38, 42, 60, 92
Sandra's artistic and innovative creations have been published in most of the major stamping magazines, as well as in her own book, *Making Gifts With Rubber Stamps* from North Light Books. She and her designs have also been seen on HGTV's *The Carol Duvall Show*. Sandra's graphic and artistic talent and her love of teaching combine to maintain her lively sense of experimentation and fun.
Sandra may be contacted at:
626-967-6527
email: McCALLSS@aol.com

Vicki Schreiner – pp. 18, 50, 58, 66, 68, 100
An artist, designer, and teacher, Vicki Schreiner has had projects and features published in many leading crafting magazines, and has appeared on *Home Matters* and QVC in the U.S., and *The Sue Warden Show* in Canada. She has written several books about woodburning and painting, and teaches the use of stamps for basic design purposes. Vicki and her daughter, Joani, are planning a book together.
Vicki may be contacted at:
417-887-9465
email: vickisoriginals@msn.com

Susan Jaworski Stranc – pp. 15, 46, 54, 62, 70, 78, 96
Among all her other creative pursuits, Susan makes marvelous, stunning handmade albums, books, and journals for sale to her many clients. Her love of all things paper is evidenced by the meticulous care that permeates her gorgeous creations. Hand painted papers, beads, intricate cutting and lacing, as well as imaginative embellishments of every type are found in Susan's creations. Each is a work of art appropriate to encase a memory or to hold a lifetime of adventures.
Susan may be contacted at:
978-465-9896
email: stranc@mediaone.net

Gallery Artists

Kari Lee – pp. 94, 103
A designer, an author and an innovator, Kari has been featured in many crafting magazines and industry trade publications. She is currently working on two books featuring the combination of rubber stamping and leather. Her beautiful and progressive design sense is in demand for television shows, classes, projects, and designs. Kari is on staff at The Leather Factory, headquartered in Fort Worth, Texas, and does freelance design work as well.
Kari may be contacted at:
The Leather Factory
713-880-8235
email: lfkari@flashnet.com

Sunn Shipton – pp. 95, 98, 99, 101, 102
Sunn Shipton and her husband Kevin own a home-based rubber stamp and ceramics company in Springvale, near Melbourne, Australia. They design and manufacture all their own stamps, which are sold under the trade name Deep Impressions and are available either mounted or unmounted. They also design and produce stamped cards and are kept very busy with their 100% homegrown business.
Sunn and Kevin Shipton may be contacted at:
Deep Impressions
Springvale, Victoria 3171
Australia
Telephone: +61-3-9574-6876
email: Impressions@hotvoice.com
or deepimpressions@hotmail.com

About the Author

Betty Auth is a freelance designer, artist, author, and editor whose interest in art and design has led her through many mediums. She designed and produced a line of cloth doll patterns and wrote regular columns for three cloth doll magazines. She generated a new interest in woodburning and wrote four books on the subject, many of the designs employing rubber stamps. Two books were written for Walnut Hollow about stamps with woodburning and stencils with woodburning. The other two are *Woodburning* for Lark Books and *The Art of Woodburning* for Sterling Publications. Betty was the consultant for a series of six books called *Remember the Years* for Fiskars, each book concentrating on a particular decade and offering time-specific papers, images, and techniques for scrapbooks. Betty has designed and published projects in the areas of quilting and appliqué, polymer clay, wire and beads, stamping, woodburning, and many others. She contributed projects to the books, *The New Photo Crafts, Fabulous Felt Crafts, Painting on Glass, Santa Claus 1999 Collection,* and *Gift Packages to Give and Give Again.* Betty has appeared on *The Carol Duvall Show* on HGTV, and was a featured artisan on *Lynette Jennings Design,* on The Discovery Channel. More than 300 of her designs have been published in national craft and general interest publications. She was the author of a regular column for *Arts & Crafts Magazine* entitled "Ready, Set, Go!" where she explored easy, intermediate, and artist projects in many mediums.

Betty has been an on-line editor and designer for a Web-based company and manages the Web site for The Society of Craft Designers. She is a finalist Craft Designer of the Year and is constantly surprised and invigorated by the creative impulse that lives within each of us. She may be contacted at: 281-879-0430; email: bauth@houston.rr.com.

Acknowledgments

Thank you to every person who has ever picked up a rubber stamp and asked, "Now, what can I do with this?" It is only through experimentation and the courage of individuals to try something new that the art of design can grow and mature.

Thank you as well to each individual who has had the desire and intention to preserve her family's photographs and to make something beautiful from them. Such efforts are a work in progress, and if you are one of those marvelous scrapbooking persons, may you never run out of photographs.

Thank you to Mary Ann Hall, Acquisitions Editor for Rockport Publishers, for the confidence and patience she has shown, first in giving me this opportunity and then in staying the course. Thanks to Judith Durant for excellence in editing and in forming my words into a cohesive whole. Thank you to Brian Piper and his staff for the photographs that helped form this volume into a real book, even over long distances and with meager notes. And thank you to all the staff at Rockport Publishers for quality in everything they do. I'm proud to be a part of it.

Dedication

This book is dedicated to my husband of a quarter-century who has watched too many television shows alone and eaten far too many tuna sandwiches when I was too busy to cook. Thanks John — let's shoot for a 50th.